Praise for Beginner

What beginners need to build confidence

"I've been trying to get good at guitar, and have actually been a builder and luthier for over 12 years, but much like Leo Fender, not a good player. This book starts at the beginning, and works it's way in, making you better and better with your fingering, which is most of the problems I have. Recommended."

— *Paul S. Brzozowski*

The Exercises Work!!

"So glad I purchased Guutar Exercises for Beginners. I feel myself getting better daily. So grateful! Thank you."

— *AB Illinois*

Great for beginners

"My son received an electric guitar for Christmas and this was a great way to get him started."

— *Melanie Magny*

Worth every penny

"Concise and clear instructions, very easy to follow. I'm a beginner guitarist, every body saying you have to practice to become better, what do you practice, the same old mistakes? This book gives clear and concise, easy to follow advise on what to practice and when. Great book helping a lot, would definitely recommend."

— *Trevor Allwright*

GUITAR EXERCISES FOR BEGINNERS

10X YOUR GUITAR SKILLS IN
10 MINUTES A DAY

GH@theguitarhead.com
www.facebook.com/theguitarhead/

Disclaimer

Dedication

We dedicate this book to the complete
Guitar Head team,
supporters, well-wishers and
the Guitar Head community.

It goes without saying that we
would not have gotten
this far without
your encouragement,
critique and support.

Table Of Contents

Free Guitar Head Bonuses

Audio Files

All Guitar Head books come with audio tracks for the licks inside the book. These audio tracks are an integral part of the book - they ensure you are playing the charts and chords the way they are intended to be played.

Lifetime access to Guitar Head Community

Being around like-minded people is the first step to being successful at anything. The Guitar Head community is a place where you can find people who are willing to listen to your music, answer your questions or talk anything guitar.

Email newsletters sent directly to your inbox

We send regular guitar lessons and tips to all our subscribers. Our subscribers are also the first to know about Guitar Head giveaways and holiday discounts.

Free PDF

Guitar mastery is all about the details! Getting the small things right and avoiding mistakes that can slow your guitar journey by years. So, we wrote a book about 25 of the most common mistakes guitarists make and decided to give it for free to all Guitar Head readers.

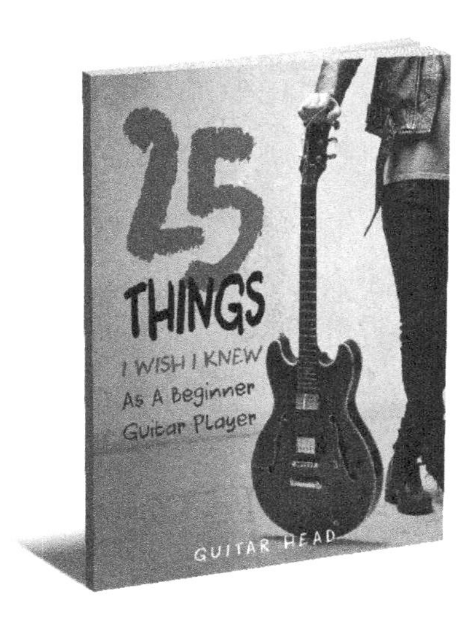

You can grab a copy of the free book, audio files and subscribe to newsletter by following the link below.

All these bonuses are a 100% free, with no strings attached. You won't need to enter any personal details other than your first name and email address.

To get your bonuses, go to: ***www.theguitarhead.com/bonus***

Note: For those interested, we have a video course for this book in which a professional guitarist explains each exercise individually. You can check it out on our website.

A note to all beginners

As you've read from the title of the book — this book has been written with an intent — to give you fun exercises to play and a simple routine to follow. To help you create a habit of practicing daily which can multiply your guitar skills.

While we've tried to include explanations to as many of the concepts as possible — at the end of the day, this book has been designed to be an "exercise book".

If you are looking for full-fledged guitar lessons for beginners — you can take a look at our book "Guitar for Beginners". There, I have enough pages and the freedom to dive deep into each topic and have full blown conversations around them.

With that said — we thank you for your trust in Guitar Head. We hope this book lives up to your expectations and becomes a valuable part of your guitar journey.

That's it — opening talk done. Let's get into the book...

Introduction

What sort of guitar player are you?

Are you the absolute beginner, who just purchased your first guitar and now you're left scratching your head, wondering what to do with it?

Are you the perpetual procrastinator? That guitar you bought years ago has done nothing but sit in its case and taunt you. "One of these days" you'll learn to play the darn thing!

Are you the frustrated "forever average" player? Maybe you've given it a fair shot — but you quickly hit a wall that has impeded any real progress?

I'm guessing that no matter what your experience level, you're reading this book because you are desperately in search of the right clues to help improve your guitar playing.

You need answers. You need discipline. You need the right system that's going to take you from **beginner** to **pro**.

Oh. And you also want to achieve this within a very reasonable time commitment.

How does 10 Minutes Per Day sound?

No, I'm not pulling your leg. That's really all it takes for most people to make incredible progress with their skills. 10 minutes of dedicated practice every day.

Think you can handle that?

I know you can!

So, crack those knuckles, buckle that guitar strap, and get ready to conquer **100 Exercises** that are laser-focused on expanding your knowledge of the guitar and dramatically improving your playing abilities.

Over the span of this book, we'll cover all the essentials:

- Reading guitar tablature
- Playing scales up and down the neck
- Mastering complete finger independence
- Understanding rhythm and different strumming patterns
- Major, Minor and Seventh chord shapes
- Advanced techniques like hammer-ons, pull-offs, and slides
- Getting you prepared to play your first songs!

So, are you ready to totally impress your friends? Are you excited to finally hit that breakthrough you've needed in your playing?

Most importantly... are you ready to prove to yourself that you've got what it takes to master the guitar?

Good.

THEN LET'S BEGIN.

CHAPTER 1

Guitar Tablature — What It Is and How to Use It

Let's clear up something right from the start:

In order to master the guitar, you do NOT have to learn how to read music.

Yep. That's right. There are plenty of famous guitarists who never learned how to formally read music. These esteemed players include Jimi Hendrix, Eric Clapton, Eddie Van Halen, and all of The Beatles.

I'm not saying learning to read music is a bad thing—it's actually quite useful to know. But you'll be relieved to hear that the guitar skills of your dreams are still attainable, without needing to decipher what all those black lines, dots and #hashtags mean.

To make things way easier, let's talk about an alternative way of noting (no pun intended) how to play the guitar. It's called **guitar tablature**, or "tab" for short.

Tablature accomplishes the same thing as formal sheet music, but it's far simpler to understand. Here it is written below, representing a famous melody:

The top section shows formal music notation—but don't stress about that. Sometimes guitar tabs include the original music notation just for your reference.

The lower section is the one we want — the one that says "TAB". You'll see that there are six lines that run horizontally across the page. Each of these lines represents one string of your guitar, with the line at the bottom representing the **6th string**, and the line at the top representing the **1st string**. Simple enough, right?

Therefore, when the guitar is on your lap, the thick string closest to you on the guitar (the 6th or **Low E** string) is the line closest to you on the TAB. And the thin string furthest from you on the guitar (the 1st or **High E** string) is the line furthest away from you on the TAB.

The numbers represent the frets that you are meant to play on the corresponding string. So easy!

There are other elements of reading tablature that are similar to music notation, such as time signatures and measures. No need to go into that now—let's just concentrate on getting the notes right first.

So, let's check it out that tab again:

If you read the tab correctly, you'll play the following notes one after the other. Also, try to use the fingers I have noted to help develop your fretting hand strength and dexterity.

- 4th string — 2nd fret (index)
- 4th string — 2nd fret (index)
- 4th string — 4th fret (ring)
- 4th string — 2nd fret (index)
- 3rd string — 2nd fret (index)
- 3rd string — 1st fret (index)

Looking at the diagram below, you'll see that each finger on your fret hand can be assigned a number:

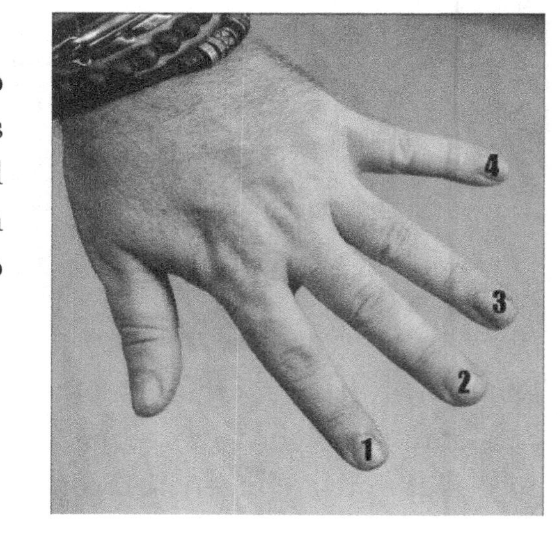

As you become more accustomed to working with guitar tabs you'll sometimes see where certain fingers are recommended to play certain notes (as we did above). In this case, the tab relates the fingers to the numbers shown:

- Index finger = 1
- Middle finger = 2
- Ring finger = 3
- Pinky finger = 4

Always try to follow the recommended fingering, as this will get you to utilize all four fingers of your fretting hand. We don't want to be locked into just a couple fingers, sloppily poking around the fret board.

A simple way to envision this is to picture a four-fret "box", with each fret being played by one finger. As your skills progress, you'll be able to change positions smoothly; it's like sliding the "box" down the fret board, using the same frame of reference of which fingers play which notes.

Once you have a good understanding of how to position your hand, practice the melody several times, taking it slow and easy.

> *Note: Check out the audio tracks included with the bonus content of this book to hear exactly how it's supposed to sound.*

Does it ring a bell? Sounds like "Happy Birthday" to me...and it will to you too once you learn to play tabs correctly!

Let's get things going with our first tab reading exercise:

Exercise #1 — Open String Tablature Exercise

This will help you understand playing open strings when you read a tab. It's also a great exercise for your picking hand to move from string to string.

In order to play this, start by picking the **open Low E** string (the thick one), then the **open A** string, then the **open D** string. Keep going and pluck the **open G** string, the **open B** string and finally the **open High E** string (the thin one).

Next, you'll reverse the movement and hit the **B** string, the **G** string, **D** string, and all the way back to where you started. Simple, yes! But a great way to get started.

Exercise #2 — Barred String Tablature Exercise

This is exactly the same motion as Exercise #1, but now you're gonna lay your index finger across the seventh fret of the guitar. Notice how the numbers have all changed from **0** to **7**, indicating that all the notes are played on the seventh fret.

Same picking pattern here: Start by plucking the **7th fret** on the **Low E** string, the **7th fret** on the **A** string, the **7th fret** on the **D** string, the **7th fret** on the **G** string, the **7th fret** on the **B** string, then the **7th fret** on the **High E** string. Then return back up to the Low E string, one string at a time.

Exercise #3 — Multi-String Tablature Exercise

Alright, I think you're ready for playing different fretted notes on different strings. This exercise is actually a C Major scale, which we'll be returning to later on.

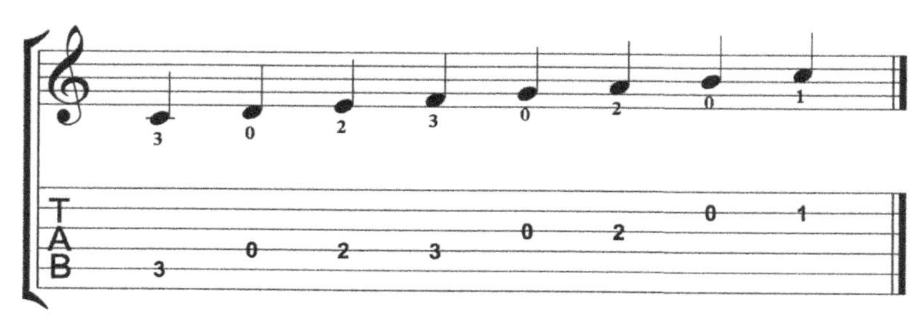

The tab above is played as follows:

1. 3rd finger on the 3rd fret of the fifth string
2. Then the open D string
3. Then the 2nd finger on the 2nd fret of the fourth string
4. And the 3rd finger on the 3rd fret of the fourth string
5. Then the open G string
6. This is followed by the 2nd finger on the 2nd fret of the third string
7. Then the open B string
8. And then finally, the 1st finger on the 1st fret of the second string

Let's be honest, our first three exercises won't have you selling out stadiums anytime soon—but they're important to practice until you can play them easily without any mistakes. This is the foundation of everything we will be covering in the rest of this book. Baby steps before ascending the "Stairway to Heaven"!

You should now have a basic understanding of tablature and be able to easily read any diagram throughout this book. More complex notation will come later, but we'll get to that when we need to.

So, let's now move on to something a bit more challenging......

Finger Independence

This is a vital skill that every guitarist must acquire, and the best and quickest way to do that is through exercises.

Every day of our lives we unconsciously utilize finger independence. Throwing a ball, holding a knife, shaking hands, typing on a keyboard—these are just some of the ways we use our fingers independently. Complete finger control is necessary for becoming adapt at the guitar; you need to be able to move one or more fingers at any time, to any position, while leaving the other fingers where they are.

Before you boast, "That's easy! Of course, I can do that," I'd like to point out this is far more difficult than it sounds. But don't fret (pun intended), I'm going to talk you through this nice and slow.

Exercise #4 — Two Finger Independence Exercise 1

We'll start with a simple two finger exercise using the index and middle fingers.

While this may look easy at first, the challenge only comes once you try playing it properly.

You're probably lifting each finger up as you play the next note, right? That's not actually how it's supposed to be played. What you need to do is play the 5th fret on the Low E string with your index finger, then *keep it in the same position* as you play the 6th fret on the same string with your middle finger.

After you've played that note, lift your 1st finger up and place it on the 5th fret of the A string and play that note. Then move the 2nd finger down a string and do the same thing.

Though this technique introduced a new challenge, if you persevere with it, you'll gain incredible finger independence, which will help make anything you learn to play on the guitar easier.

> *TIP: Remember that one of the keys to making this easy to play and sound good is to use the correct hand position around the neck — and to use your fingertips, not the edge of your fingers, to play the notes.*

Exercise #5 — Two Finger Independence Exercise 2

The next exercise is a variation on the one we've just covered, but we're now using the 1st and 3rd fingers. Again, remember to keep your index finger held down while playing the second note to get the most benefit from this exercise.

Exercise #6 — Two Finger Independence Exercise 3

Now let's step it up by introducing your weakest finger, the pinky, and see how that gets on.

Don't hurt yourself

If you experience any pain in your pinky, don't power on through it—this isn't the gym. Your fingers need to become accustomed to the tasks you're now putting them through, and pain could be a sign that something isn't right with your technique...

This may be incorrect hand positioning. Try adjusting your wrist so it's in a straighter position. It should be firm, but not completely locked and rigid. Remember also to have your fingertips press on the strings at as close to a 90-degree angle as you can.

It could also be your body telling you that you're pushing it too far; this is especially true if you feel your hand warming up. If that's the case, take a break from your practice session and come back later. Whatever you do, don't keep pushing; you could strain something severely and be out of practice for weeks while your hand recovers.

Exercise #7 — Two Finger Independence Exercise 4

Let's switch it up and get your other fingers working together. The following exercise will train your middle and ring fingers to work independently of each other. For variety sake, let's play this starting from the 3rd fret.

Exercise #8 — Two Finger Independence Exercise 5

Next up, let's see how your middle and your little finger work together. We'll start on the 5th fret for this one, which is a standard "home" position for many scales and solos.

Exercise #9 — Two Finger Independence Exercise 6

Finally, it's up to the 7th fret. Let's have your teensy-weensy ring ringer and pinky finger share a dance together! Quite a workout, huh?

This concludes our finger pair independence exercises. But before we move on to the three finger versions, let's take a slight detour and discuss picking.

Alternate vs. Economy Picking

There are a number of ways that you can pick guitar strings, but the two most established and widely used methods are **alternate picking** and **economy picking**.

When most beginners start off, the most natural way to pick a string is by using a *downstroke*. There's nothing fundamentally wrong with this—in fact, many fantastic riffs from famous bands are played using this technique, i.e. Metallica and Black Sabbath.

However, it isn't very efficient if you need to play a lot of notes quickly and smoothly. In order to do that you need to adopt one of the more complicated picking techniques—and by far the most common is alternate picking...

Alternate Picking

With alternate picking, you're performing a picking motion of down-*up-down-up* or *up-down-up-down*. Quite simply, you play the first note with a downstroke, then the second with an upstroke, then the third with a downstroke and the fourth with an upstroke, regardless of what string the notes are on.

However, if you're playing an exercise that has three notes per string, you would pick the first note down, the next up, and the next down — all on the same string. Then you'd move the plectrum to the next string and continue the same pattern.

Here is Exercise #3 again using ⊓ to indicate downstrokes and V to indicate upstrokes.

Notice that, for the second note, you move over the string with your plectrum and then pick it using an upstroke. This is a much more fluid way to play than by plucking every note with downstrokes. I strongly recommend that you use it for all the exercises in this book until it becomes second nature.

Once you get the hang of it you can then opt for the more complicated Economy picking method when the situation calls for it.

Economy Picking

Economy picking involves using the most convenient picking order depending on the particular riff or scale you're playing. Unlike with alternate picking, this method allows you to move your pick between strings by using two downstrokes or upstrokes in a row if that's the most efficient way to get to the next note.

Here's the same example again, but using Economy Picking:

Yeah, it's gonna feel a bit goofy until you get the hang of it. If it makes you feel any better, there are many legendary guitarists who hardly ever use economy picking and choose instead to play more than 99% of their songs, riffs and solos using only alternate picking.

For this reason, it's generally a best practice to always use the standard alternate picking method, unless it's somehow easier to change strings by doing two down or up strokes in succession.

OK, let's return to the exercises...

Exercise #10 — Three Finger Independence Exercise 1

Since I just introduced you to alternate picking, I'll indicate it on the next few exercises so you can start to become familiar with it. However, I won't be doing it for the whole book, because once you get the hang of it, it should become second nature. Just remember to keep doing it on every exercise.

This is our first three finger independence exercise, which is basically the same as the two finger exercises, we've already covered, but obviously using three fingers.

The same principles and techniques apply here. Remember to always keep your fingers in position on the fretboard until you need to move them. Lifting your fingers after every note may be easier—but it will slow down your development!

Exercise #11 — Three Finger Independence Exercise 2

Next up we're going to incorporate our first, second and pinky fingers together. Let's play it starting from the 7th fret to keep things fresh.

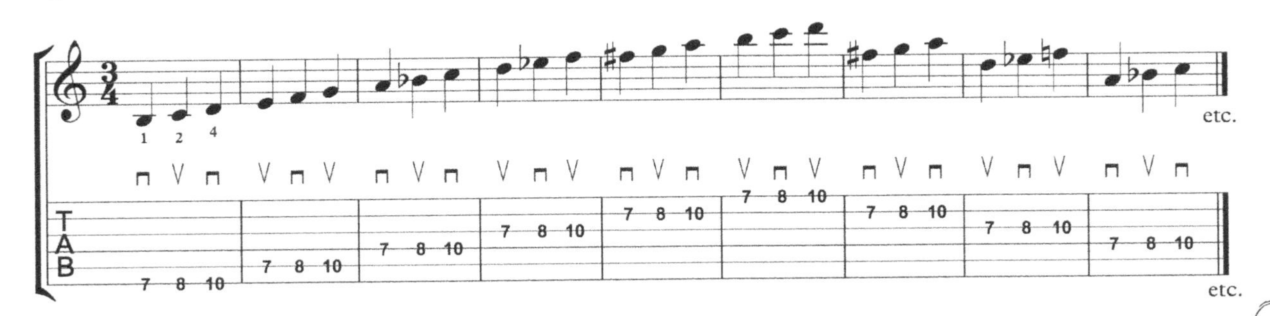

Exercise #12 — Three Finger Independence Exercise 3

Basically, the same pattern, but this time using our 1st, 3rd, and 4th fingers. Back to the 5th fret for this one.

Exercise #13 — Three Finger Independence Exercise 4

Here's something your hands probably aren't used to—a middle finger, ring finger and pinky finger exercise!

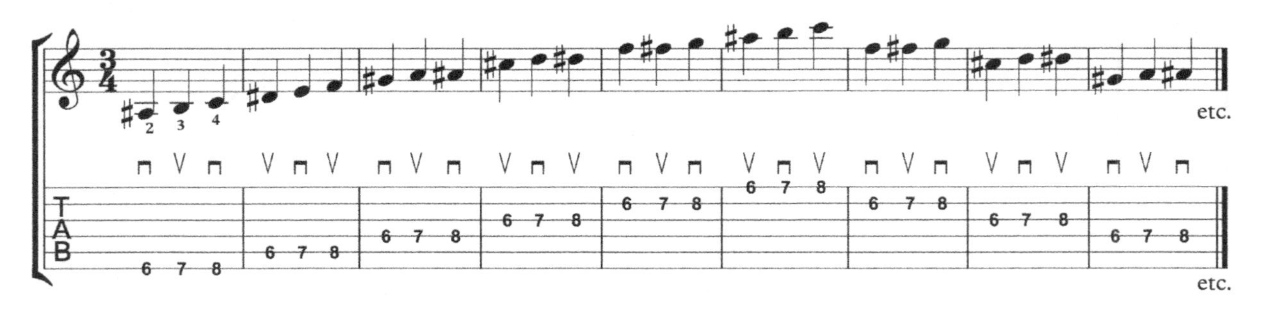

Exercise #14 — The Four Finger Independence Exercise

To finish off our section on Finger Independence, here's the big daddy of them all: the four-finger independence exercise.

This is one of the best exercises there is; many professional guitarists even continually use it as a warmup for their practice sessions and live concerts. The smoother, faster, and more in control you get with it, the better a guitarist you will become.

To start with, play it slowly and steadily. Concentrate on getting every note to sound perfect. Don't rush! Over time and with concentrated practice, you will naturally play it faster while still retaining crystal clear precision. And as with all the exercises in this book, remember to use alternate picking throughout.

Lock that one away in your practice toolbox. You've now graduated from the Finger Independence exercises!

But before we move on to the more physically and mentally exerting exercises, let's discuss the nature of practice in a little more detail...

The Art of Practice

If you learn to practice properly and efficiently, you will see continual growth in your guitar playing. In fact, if you practice properly then it's *impossible* to stagnate, and you will surely get better as every day passes.

So how much time should you practice every day?

You may be pleasantly surprised to learn that it really only takes 10 minutes of practice every day to see noticeable improvement. (OK, maybe you're not surprised — you know the title of this book, after all!)

This has to be concentrated effort, though—and everything needs to be broken down into small, achievable sections that will guarantee your progress. That's why the exercises in this book are so effective they give you actionable and focused goals to hit for your every-day practice sessions.

The art of "proper" practice comes down to three important factors:

Challenge Yourself

For a practice session to be beneficial, you have to constantly push yourself to play things that you don't already know or can't play well enough.

There is absolutely no point sitting down with a guitar and playing the same chord progression for the thousandth time for 10 minutes and think that you have practiced. You have not. And you are no better at the end of that 10-minute session than you were at the beginning.

That's not to say that you can't improve on songs that you are not playing well enough. But during your practice time, you should analyze which sections you can't play well enough and ONLY concentrate on them.

For example, there may be a difficult chord change you're having trouble with. If so, spend a few minutes repeating it until it becomes easier. That will do you a lot more good than playing through the entire song for five minutes when the chord change only occurs a few times in the whole song.

If you want to play the song in full, go ahead. Enjoy it. But do that for pleasure, and OUTSIDE of your 10 minutes of scheduled practice.

1. Concentration is the Key

The second factor is absolute concentration. Split whatever you're going to practice up into short time frames — three minutes is the standard that most guitarists stick to. This will give you three 3-minute blocks to practice anything you like within each practice session, plus a minute to rest and prepare for the next exercise.

If, for example, you decide that you're going to incorporate the four finger independence exercise into your practice routine (which I strongly recommend), then you first allocate three minutes of your schedule to that exercise. For those three minutes only, all you'll be doing is playing that exercise as perfectly as you can.

So, yes, that means you'll need to invest in a stopwatch. Or use one on your phone. Or I guess watch the minute hand on your grandfather clock.

Either way, timing is essential. Which brings us to our last factor for effective practicing...

2. Watch Your Timing

You will also need a metronome. This again can be a stand-alone model, or you can use any of the downloadable metronome apps that are freely available for your smartphone.

Set the metronome to a very slow setting, most guitarists start off at 60 BPM. You don't play on every beat of the metronome, however; you play on *every other*. This ensures that you learn to be perfectly in time.

Most people have a "natural" timing, which may either be slightly before, on, or slightly after the beat. You need to work on aligning to *perfect* timing, not natural timing, so that everything you play is rhythmically where it should be.

If, for example, you play on every beat and are ever-so-slightly ahead or behind the beat, you will never notice, because you are always that tiny bit out. On the other hand, if you play on every *other* beat, the one that you don't play on naturally sets you in time, ensuring absolute accuracy.

Back to the Exercises...

OK, so you're going to play the four-finger independence exercise for three minutes, and you're going to time it with a metronome set to 60 BPM, and you're going to play on every other beat. Great!

... But here's where you're going to become impatient. You're gonna think it feels extremely slow. And you know what? It is! But it needs to be.

It is crucial that when you practice you are playing absolutely perfectly — and not reinforcing mistakes or bad technique. Every note has to be picked exactly in time with the metronome. You have to use precise alternate picking. No note is allowed to rattle, and each one must be crystal clear.

All of this requires great care and precision—and you'll lose that if you're practicing too fast when starting out. So, shake those ants out of your pants! You gotta slow it down and take your time.

However, if after only a few days you're managing to play it perfectly, you can then increase the metronome speed to, say, 63 BPM. Practice that for a few days, and then increase it again—maybe to 67 BPM. This method allows you to very gradually increase the speed — but without sacrificing precision.

In a few months, your hands will be *flying* around the guitar—but not in some random mess They will be deliberate and precise. *That's* what practicing properly can do for you.

Practice, practice, practice — but do it <u>properly</u>!

So please take the time to practice properly. Yes, it will seem very slow and even tedious when starting out—but just like going to the gym, as soon as you start seeing the results, nothing will stop you. Playing the guitar becomes easier and more fun the more you improve. Just stick with it and trust in the process.

Exercise #15 — The Spider

Here's another favorite exercise amongst the pros. It's affectionately known as the "spider" because your hand will walk up and down the neck with the fluidity of an acrobatic arachnid.

As with all the exercises, start slowly, use alternate picking and make sure every note is played perfectly and rings true.

The concept behind it is that you play a specific four-note sequence, then repeat that sequence for the next four notes—but starting on the *second* note of the sequence and finishing on the *first*. Then you repeat again, but this time start on the *third* note and finish on the *second*... Lastly, you start on the fourth note and finish on the third note.

Sounds complicated (and it is!), but once you get your fingers working, it'll make a lot more sense.

Here it is in tablature:

Now that was fun, wasn't it? What makes this exercise particularly useful is that it improves the connection between your brain and your fingers, allowing you to play whatever's on your mind with more control. In fact, it's probably the *best* exercise there is for doing that!

But that's only the beginning. Let's take it a step further...

Exercise #16 — The Reverse Spider

Even more of a head scratcher. Here's the fun-loving spider in reverse!

From here on it's basically up to you to invent increasingly more complicated versions of the spider walk. The purpose is to stretch your mental capabilities and improve the transfer of information from your brain to your fingers.

It's helpful to write your custom sequences on a piece of paper first to use as reference. For example, 1-3-4-2, 3-4-2-1, 4-2-1-3, 2-1-3-4, and repeat. Once you're comfortable and confident with the order, it'll be locked into your muscle memory without the need for the paper.

Endorsed by a Guitar Legend

Guitar virtuoso Steve Vai actually used this exercise as one of his main improvement techniques when he was studying and learning his craft. His thinking behind it was that if he could play patterns as complicated as any that could be devised, then playing any regular song would be easy in comparison.

So, let's finish off with one even more complicated version — then you'll be on your own from here on.

Exercise #17 — The Confusing Spider

Here goes, try and get your head around this one...

That's enough brain drain for now. Let's move on to another important aspect of guitar playing, which has more to do with your hands than your brain...

Exercise #18 — Finger Strength 1

Having sufficient finger strength is an obvious an advantage, regardless of what you're playing on the guitar. But how do you make your fingers stronger? Do you make them do press-ups? Well... um... yes. Yes, you do.

Starting position Exercise

This might look a little confusing in the diagram, but it's actually quite straightforward. You start the exercise with your 1st finger on the fifth fret of the D string, your 2nd finger on the sixth fret of the D string, your 3rd finger on the seventh fret of the G string, and your 4th on the eighth fret of the G string. This is referred to as the **starting position**.

What you're going to do is lift your middle finger, and then place it back in the same position over and over again until the exercise is over. Again, this is normally done as a warmup exercise and usually for three minutes—but due to its simplicity, you can perform it at higher metronome speeds starting at around 90 BPM. Remember to alternate pick throughout!

Don't overlook this one because of how simple and easy it is. It's a great way to quickly increase the strength of your fingers.

Exercise #19 — Finger Strength 2 — Variations

This exercise can be played in five other variations. Here's the first one:

Starting position Exercise

Same as the original, but now we're using our 2nd and 3rd fingers to do the press-ups.

The next variation involves using the 3rd and 4th fingers in the same way.

> *Be careful about causing strain. If you feel your fingers getting hot — STOP! Regardless of how long you've done the exercise, you can easily strain your little finger if you're not careful.*

Exercise #20 — Finger Strength 3 — Extended Finger Pairs

The last three variations involve extended finger pairs. The first is shown below:

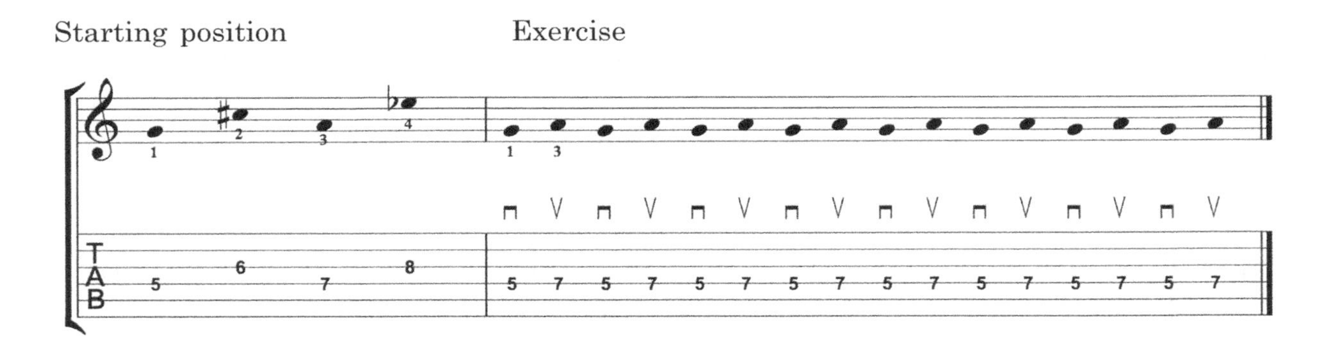

Again, basically the same exercise as Exercise 18, but this time using your 1st and 3rd fingers to do the press-ups.

The next variation uses the 2nd finger and 4th. And the final variation uses the 1st and 4th fingers.

Again, don't strain yourself. I know, I know — I sound like a worried parent. But this can be an intense exercise for fingers that have likely never worked this hard before.

Exercise #21 — Finger Stretch 1

Now we're going to strettttttch your fretting hand. Yoga pants not required.

This is done by using your 1st finger to play the first note on the 5th fret of the low E string, then using your 2nd finger to play the 7th fret of the same string, before repeating as you go through the other strings. Don't forget to use a metronome and alternate picking!

Due to the difficulty of this exercise, it's recommended that you start by first "jumping" slightly between the notes as you play them, to slowly increase the reach of your fingers. As your hand becomes more limber, you can try playing them while keeping the 1st finger down as you play the 2nd finger.

Exercise #22 — Finger Stretch 2 — Variations

In exactly the same way as with the Finger Strength Exercises, you can now adapt this exercise to be played on your other fingers. Here is an example using the 2nd and 3rd fingers playing the sixth and eighth frets respectively.

This could then be adapted for using the 3rd and 4th fingers.

Another variation involves stretching the fingers across three frets, but this is different and does involve a little "jumping" between the notes.

Exercise #23 — Finger Stretch 3 — Extended Finger Pairs

Again, like the Finger Strength Exercises, these stretching exercises can also be played with extended finger pairs. This example uses the 1st and 3rd fingers playing the fifth and eighth frets.

If after a while it gets quite easy, try using the fifth and ninth frets to challenge yourself.

This can then be played using the 2nd and 4th fingers. The final variation uses the 1st and 4th fingers across the fifth and the ninth, tenth or even the eleventh or twelfth fret—if you can manage it.

Technical Exercises Conclusion

That brings us to the end of our first batch of the technical exercises!

You must be thinking: "How on earth am I going to fit all that into my daily practice routine??"

Well, even though there are a massive number of variations covered in these Finger Independence, Spider, Finger Strength and Finger Stretch exercises — you obviously don't need to work on every one every day. That would take several hours, instead of 10 minutes.

Therefore, I recommend you just focus on one of each per day. So, on Day 1, do either a Finger Independence or Spider exercise, followed by a Finger Strength, followed by a Finger Stretch. Then on Day 2, do a different set of exercises, so that you are exercising all the fingers and finger pairs.

However, the one problem with this system is that you won't really build blistering speed on a single exercise. If that's your aim, it's recommended to choose a speed exercise; for example, one of the spiders every day, increasing the metronome speed until your fingers are flying around the fretboard. (Be sure to supplement the speed exercise with one finger strength and stretch exercise on a daily basis.)

> *"If you want to be a rock star or just be famous, then run down the street naked, you'll make the news or something. But if you want music to be your livelihood, then play, play, play and play! And eventually, you'll get to where you want to be."*
>
> *Eddie Van Halen*

CHAPTER 2

Let's Play Some Melodies

Melodies are the fundamentals of music. In simple terms, melody can be defined as a sequence of notes that is musically satisfying. When you hum or whistle along to a tune you can't remember the words to, it's the melody that remains stuck in your head.

I'm sure you didn't pick up the guitar so you could play the spider walk endlessly. Melodies are what you're here for—so let's start off by learning some simple ones.

Perhaps no melody is more well-known than our first one, the ever-popular "Happy Birthday".

Exercise #24 — Happy Birthday Melody

You've heard it. I've heard it. We all know what it sounds like. This is a great exercise to start off with, because you'll know immediately if you're playing it wrong.

As with the earlier technical exercises, always use alternate picking to create a smoother and more dynamic feel.

Exercise #25 — Old McDonald Had a Farm Melody

Another one everybody knows. Notice that the first four bars are repeated once, before moving to the next melody starting at measure five:

You then return to the first melody to finish the song off. Nice and simple (and agricultural!)

Exercise #26 — Jingle Bells Chorus Melody

OK, let's trade the farmyard and cowbells for festiveness and sleighbells as we tackle this Christmas classic.

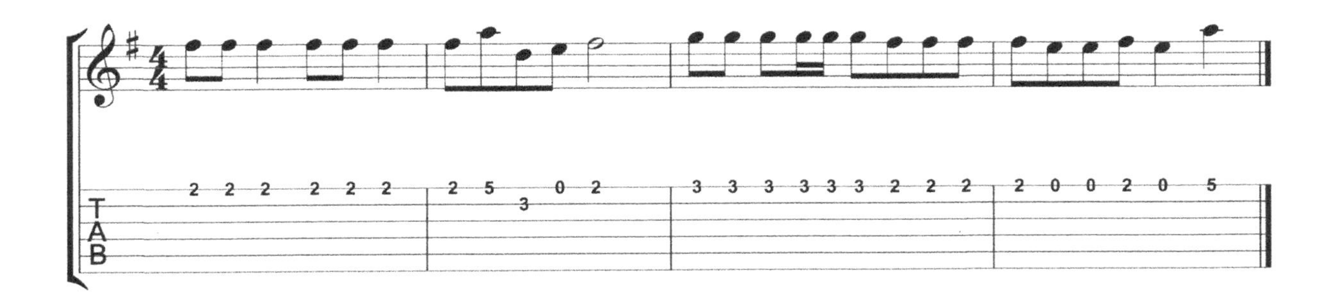

Exercise #27 — Goodnight Ladies

Next up we have 'Goodnight Ladies,' an American folk song attributed to Edwin Pearce Christy that was based on his 1847 song 'Farewell, Ladies.' The version of the song known today was first published on May 16, 1867.

In the 9th bar of the chorus, the melody is the same as that of 'Mary Had A Little Lamb.' Here is a simplified version of the song for you.

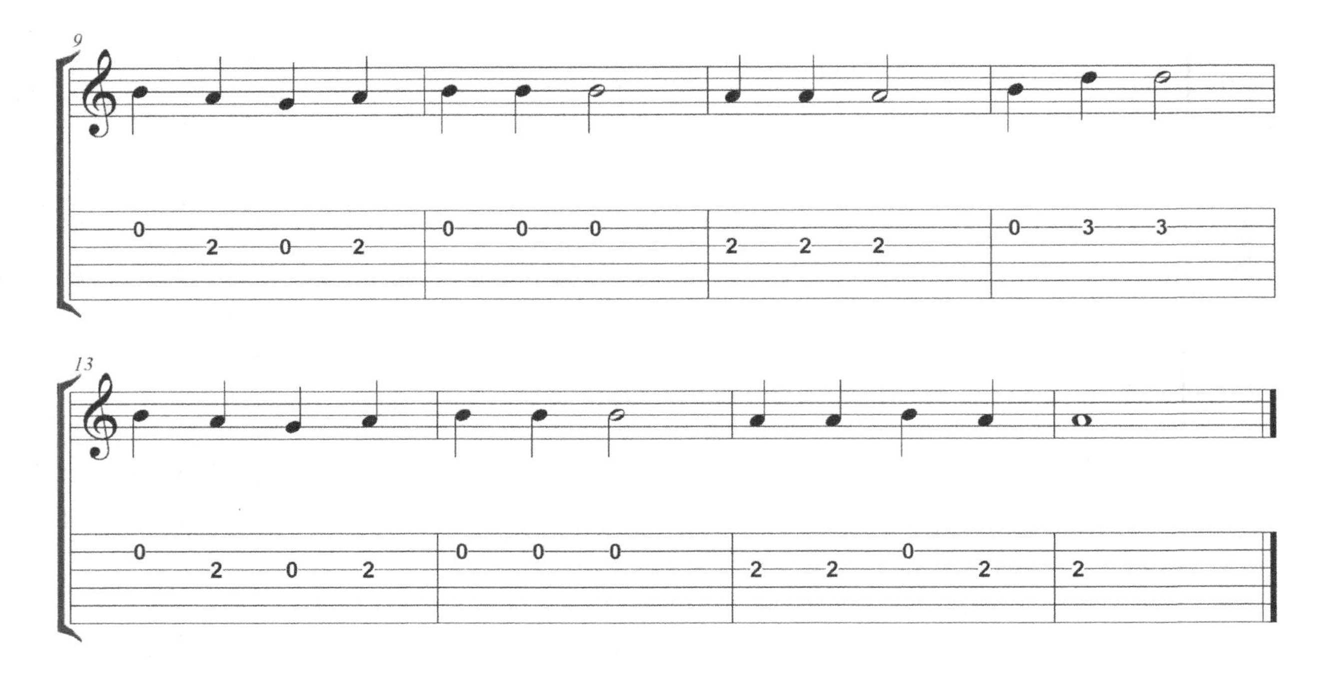

Exercise #28 — Aura Lea Melody

"Aura Lea", which is often spelled as "Aura Lee", is an American Civil War song about a maiden. It was written by W.W. Fosdick and George R. Poulton. The melody was borrowed by Elvis Presley for his 1956 hit song "Love Me Tender".

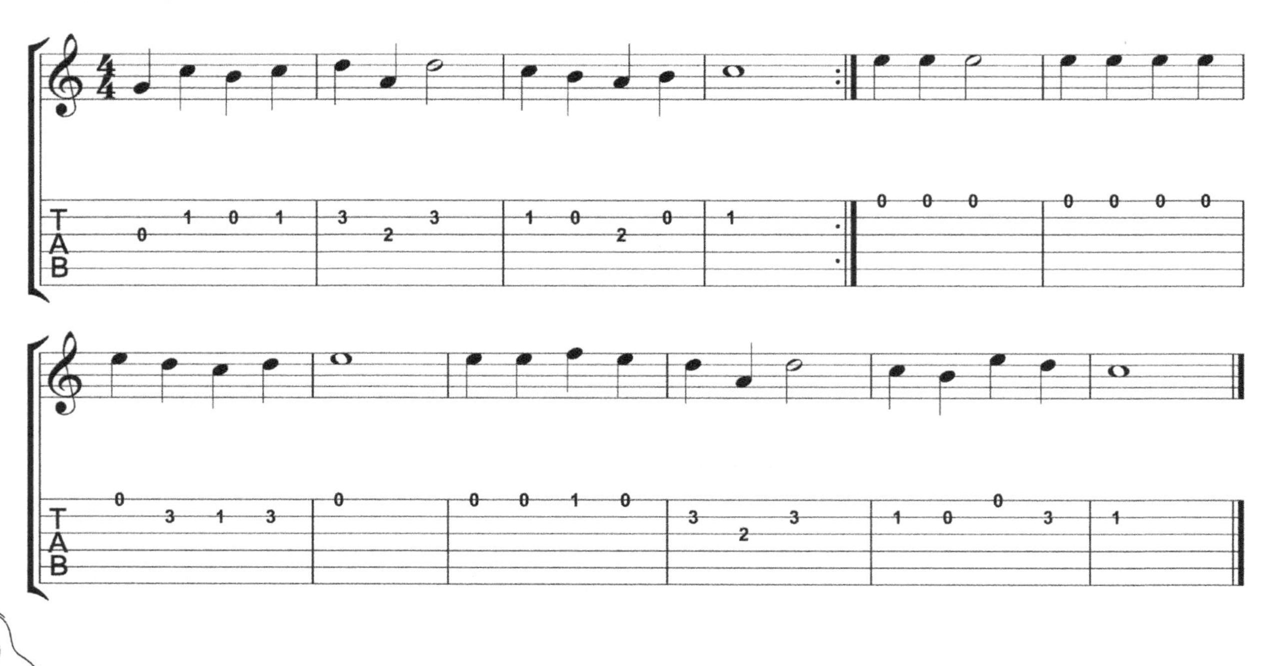

Exercise #29 — Amazing Grace Melody

"Amazing Grace" is a Christian hymn written in 1772 by the English poet and Anglican clergyman John Newton. It was published in 1779.

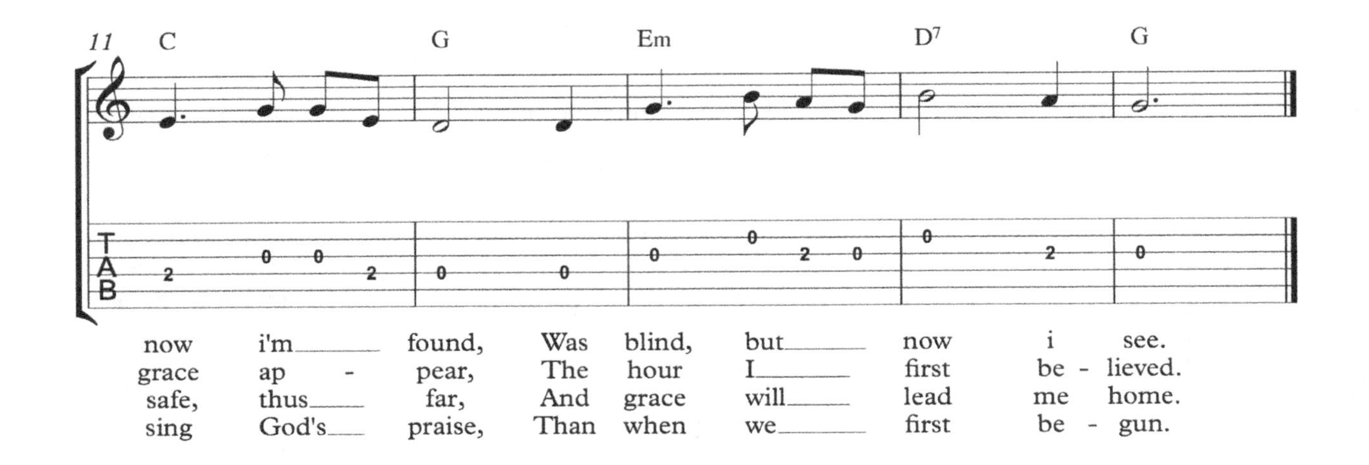

> *"Music is a necessity. After food, air, water, and warmth, music is the next necessity of life."*
>
> *Keith Richards, Rolling Stones*

CHAPTER 3

Let's Play Some Chords

As you've no doubt gathered, learning the guitar is about more than just playing single notes. There are also **chords** to learn!

Chords can be thought of as the building blocks of music. They form the backbone of a song's structure when played as themselves—or even as melodies when playing the individual notes within them.

Chords are played by fretting certain notes across three or more strings at the same time. To keep things simple, we're going to start by only learning three chords.

Why only three? Because that's all you need to play a *ton* of songs using very simple sequences. The chords we are going to work on are called:

A major, **D major**, and **E major**.

As a side note, chords can be either "major" or "minor". At this stage, all you need to know is that major chords typically sound *happy, whereas* minor chords sound *sad*. It is a mix of both that gives a song its "feel".

There's an important distinction to be aware of between notes and chords. For example, there is a D chord and a D note. The difference is that with a chord there are several different notes played together to create a combined sound, whereas with a note there is only the single tone.

Here's some guitar tab with the chords we're focused on:

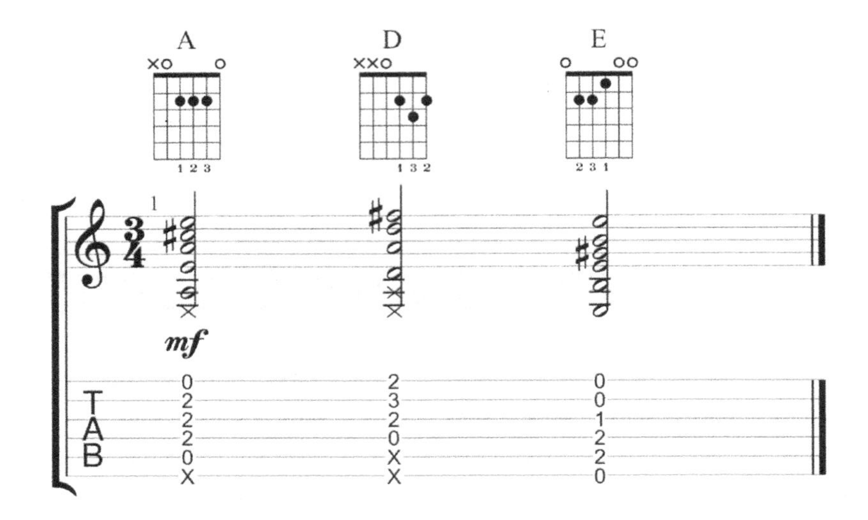

The top section shows another way you'll see chords written out, in the form of chord diagrams. These graphical representations show you where on the fretboard they're played, as well as which finger to use for each note. Each horizontal line represents a fret, each vertical line a string, and each circle shows the note that needs to be played. Underneath that line/ string is a number that corresponds to the right finger.If you see or write a single capital letter, it means you're referring to a major chord. For example, a simple "E" in a chord diagram would mean the E major chord, and a "D" would mean the D major chord.

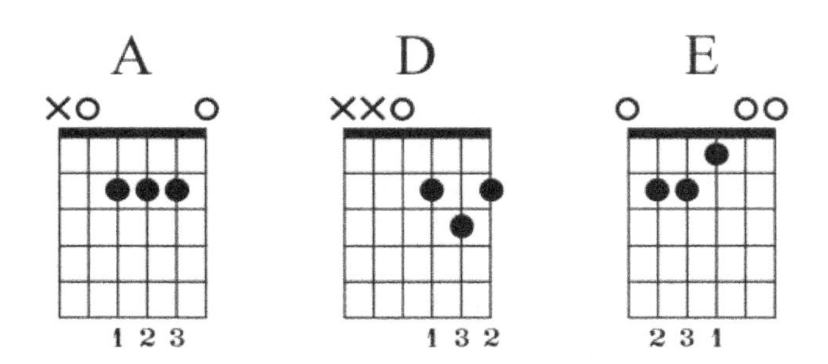

Let's practice each chord individually first so that you can get your fingers in exactly the right places. I'd suggest starting out with the simple A Major (A). Then you can continue with D Major (D), and then the E Major (E).

This is what your finger placement should look like on the fretboard:

A Major (A)

D Major (D)

E Major (E)

Things to Look Out For

To play the chords, the only thing we need to do is to sweep our pick across the strings, playing them all in the same stroke. This is called a "strum".

Getting all the notes to sound nice and clear when you play any of these chords is very difficult at first. This is why we start out by practicing Finger Strength exercises. So, don't rush and be patient.

Concentrate on getting every note to produce an un-muffled sound. It will require some force and pressure for your fingers to press hard enough to get a decent sound.

It's likely that your other fingers may be slightly touching the string you're playing, which will dampen it and produce a deadened sound. This is particularly common with the D chord and A chord.

Once you've checked that each note sounds good on its own, now strum the whole chord. When you're happy and comfortable with the sound, move on to the next chord.

Don't Get Frustrated!

OK. I need to tell you that it's really, REALLY important not to let yourself get too frustrated. Playing chords can be tough—and this is often where most beginner guitarists give up.

Rarely will a beginner get it right the first time out. I'm just being honest. It's a challenge. But practice makes perfect, right? Even Steve Vai started somewhere.

Let's look at some things that commonly can go wrong—because if you know what to look for, you'll be able to straighten them out and get cleaner sound in much less time.

I imagine the first time you tried the chord; you probably got a "plunky" (it's a real word now, remember?) sound, rather than a clear chord sound.

This is probably because your fingers are touching everywhere except where they're supposed to, which is causing the notes to become muted.

Consequently, you may be asking yourself:

"Are my fingers too fat?"

Don't laugh! I've honestly heard many people say this...

Nope — your fingers are absolutely fine! You're just not holding the chord correctly.

Playing chords requires you to hold the guitar in a particular way, and that varies slightly from player to player because we all have different sized hands and fingers. You might get away with sloppy posture if you're playing single string tunes, but that unrefined style quickly reveals itself when you start playing chords.

You should be pressing on the strings with the very tip of your fingers, and they should be perpendicular to the fretboard. Also, try curling your palm inwards to get a better grip around the neck.

Trial and Error

It's all about trial and error until you find the sweet spot. Hold the chord, try picking each string individually to see if they ring properly. If they don't ring out, you need to adjust whichever finger is causing the problem. When they do ring out, try to remember that hand position and build muscle memory.

It's important to realize that what may be the "perfect" hand position for one chord may not work for another one. Just as the fingering patterns for each chord are different, you also will need to make subtle adjustments to your wrist and hand position so that it feels comfortable and sounds clear.

I can already sense your growing frustration. Promise me you'll take your time with this! It's like good barbecue... low and slow will give you the best results.

Once you've gotten all three of these chords down, we can move on to bigger and better things. Playing chords correctly is great—but it doesn't mean jack squat unless you string them together to play a song.

Now, let's move on to...

Chord Progressions — Let's Join Those Chords Together!

Now that you can play these chords with ease and confidence, your next task is to put them in a specific sequence, which is commonly called a "chord progression".

Did you know that every song you've ever heard (no, I'm not exaggerating), yes, every one ever written is comprised of chords? And you'll be amazed by how many of them are made up of A, D, and E.

Many beginner guitarists don't realize this fact. They hear someone playing a killer guitar solo and think that's what true guitar playing is all about. Well, no it isn't. Not by a long shot. 99% of a song is how its chord progression is structured.

Learning to play some common chords is a worthy accomplishment. But stringing them together smoothly and in the right sequence is how real music is made.

So, without further ado...

Mastering the Shift

One of the most important skills for any guitarist to master is the ability to shift between chords at will. There's very little else that will dramatically improve your dexterity than by working on this skill.

Shifting between chords quickly and easily is a necessity for most popular songs. Here we'll start by learning a very common chord progression that's found in loads of popular tunes. I think you'll be pretty surprised as to how many songs you can play once you get it nailed.

The chord progression is as follows: **A — D — E — A** (which is actually, **A major**, **D major**, **E major**, and **A major**).

Exercise #30 — Chord Progression 1

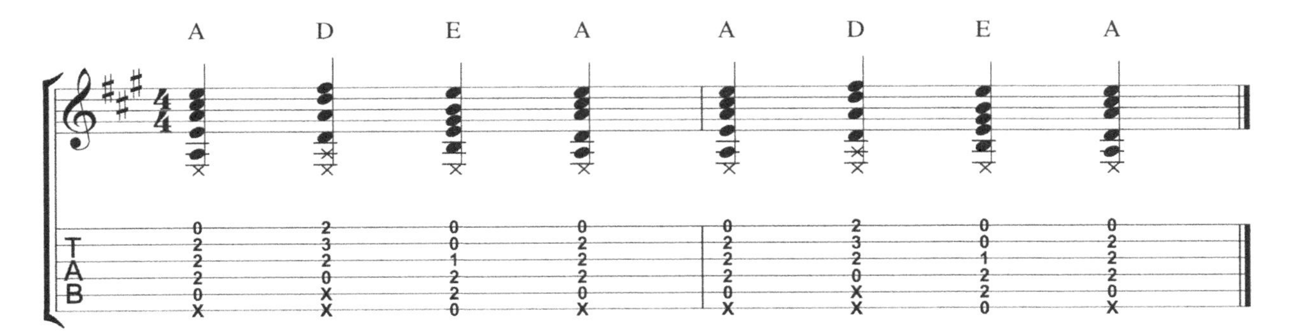

I've got three tips for you to make things a little easier. Everyone can get by with a little help from their friends, right?

Right!

Anticipate

The first important rule is to try to stay ahead of the curve. When you're playing a chord, always be thinking of the next one in the progression. Visualizing the chord on the fretboard before you shift to it is a great mental exercise.

Minimize Movement

This second tip will make you ultra-efficient when it comes to moving your fingers. One thing that most beginners tend to do is "clear" the fretboard as they are going from one chord to the next, completely removing their hand and fingers from the neck.

What we want to do is minimize the distance the hand must travel on the fretboard. It's a fraction of a second that we're talking here, but it's enough to make the music sound sloppy. Always strive to keep your fingers as close to the fretboard as possible at all times.

Slide into It!

It's definitely a challenge to quickly place three fingers on the fretboard at three precisely different places. If only there was a simpler way! Well, there is. Try

Let's take the change from an E chord to a D chord for example.

First of all, play an E chord. You'll notice that your 1st finger is on the first fret of the third string (G). Now, lift your 2nd and 3rd fingers off the fretboard, but leave the 1st finger where it is.

Then slide your 1st finger up to the second fret. Immediately put your 2nd finger on the second fret of the first string (E) and add your 3rd finger on the third fret of the second string (B). You've got a D chord!

So, give it a strum and give yourself a pat on the back. But don't drop your guitar! On second thought, just keep your hands where they are.

Anyway... now, lift the 2nd and 3rd fingers, leaving the 1st finger in place, and slide it back to the first fret. Put the other two fingers down to make an E chord again. Repeat this change until it becomes easy.

The note that slides between the chords acts as an anchor, so your other fingers know what they have to do and where they have to go. This is one of the biggest secrets in learning to change between the chords quickly in the early stages, but you can still apply the technique through all your years of playing.

Here are some exercises that this concept:

Exercise #31 — Slide into It 1 — E to D to E

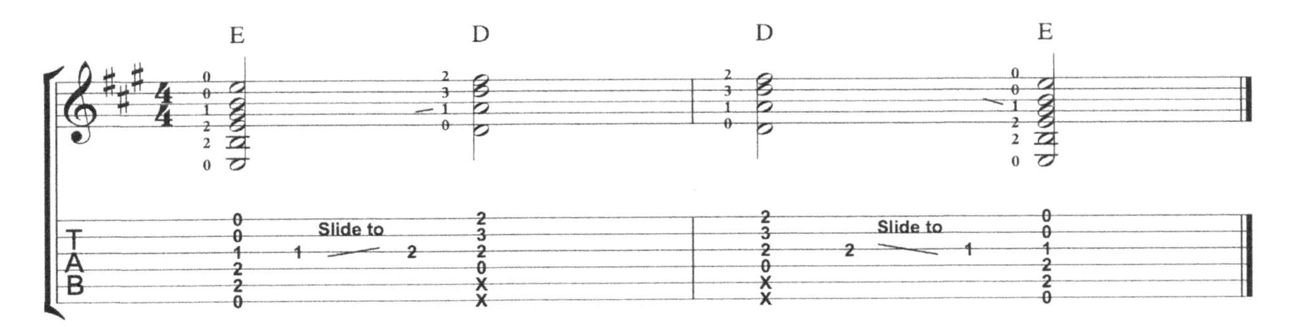

Here's what we've covered above. It's all about that 1st finger slide between the first and second fret.

Exercise #32 — Slide into It 2 — D to A to D

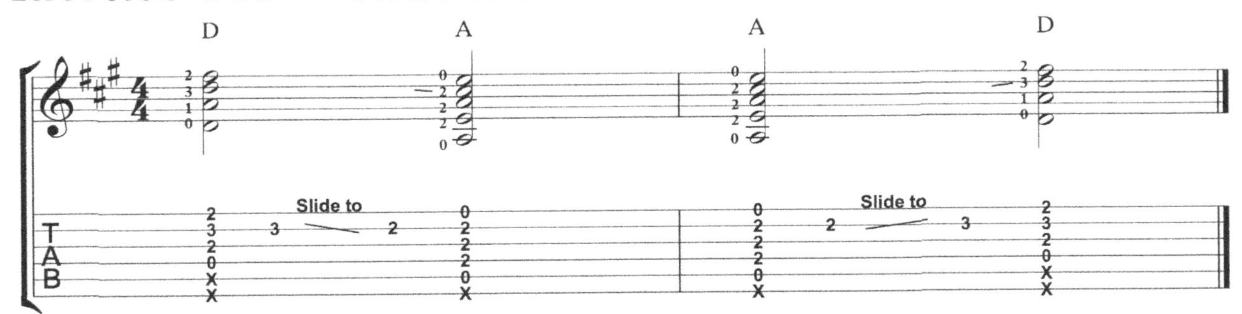

The same thing applies when changing from a D to an A, but this time the 3rd finger is the anchor.

Play the D chord as normal, then lift your 1st and 2nd fingers off, but leave the 3rd finger where it is. Now slide the 3rd finger back one fret and put your other two fingers above it on the fretboard — and you've got an A chord. Give it a strum!

Next, take the 1st and 2nd fingers back off the fretboard, and slide the 3rd finger back up a fret. Put the 1st and 2nd fingers back on, and you're back playing a D chord! Again, repeat the change until it becomes second nature.

Exercise #33 — Slide into It 3 — A to D to E to D to A

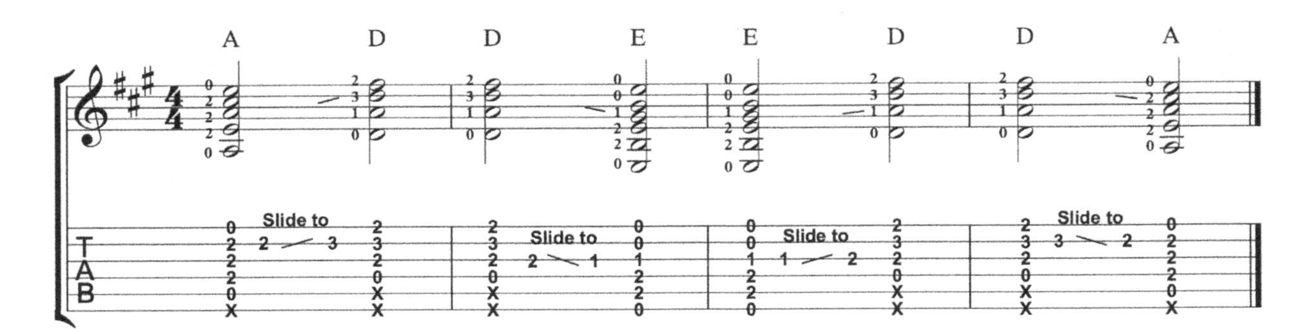

You must be getting the hang of this by now, so I won't give a full explanation of how to do this one. Simply follow the diagram, then practice it over and over until you play it like a pro!

BTW: There is no slide that will take you from an E chord to an A chord, so you'll have to lift all three fingers for that chord change.

The Chord Shift

In order to nail this chord progression, you'll need to practice each chord combination separately.

Start by playing A, then play a D, remembering to use the sliding technique. Then practice going to E, again remembering to slide your first finger. Then E back to A. Make sure you isolate each shift and practice them until you can play each one relatively easily.

Once you've gotten "all shifty" and stuff, it's time to put everything together. Since we haven't really talked about strumming yet, let's keep it simple for now.

Play a chord by striking all the strings with the pick in one motion (also known as "strumming", as we mentioned before), then count to 4 and change the chord.

Imagine counting 1-2-3-4,1-2-3-4... continuously at the same tempo. Strum the A chord by hitting all strings as you say "1" — then count "2,3,4." Change to D as you say "1" out loud. Strum again and repeat this for the entire sequence. Then start the progression again from the A chord.

Remember what I said: Most beginners give up at this point.

But you won't be one of them, right??

Slow and steady wins the race, folks. I know you're getting anxious about strumming chords at the pace of a tortoise. You want to immediately take off and start riffing like John Mayer or Jimi Hendrix.

Well, only with motivation and determination will you get there. And you've gotta hone the fundamentals before you go anywhere. Trust in the process.

In the words of the legendary guitarist...

> *"The beautiful thing about learning is nobody can take it away from you."*
>
> *B. B. King*

CHAPTER 4

Getting Rhythmic with Time Signatures

It's all in the timing.

Now that you can string chords together and shift from one to the other, you're ready to incorporate the right timing and rhythm.

Set the Beat

Have you ever found yourself tapping your foot or nodding your head to your favorite tune?

If so, congratulations — you just found the tempo of the song!

Everything in rhythm is related to the tempo of a song. For most music, the tempo determines the length of the most basic rhythmic figure, which is called a **quarter note**. This can also be referred to as the basic beat. Therefore, one tap of your foot equals one quarter note or one **beat**. In most songs, there are four beats to a bar.

If a bar contains four beats (or, in this case, four quarter notes), then when you tap your foot in rhythm to a song four times, you will be tapping out a whole bar. This is what's called 4/4 time — or "common time".

A bar can be split in any number of ways. The four quarter notes we just covered is one of them, but these can also be subdivided to make eight **8th notes**. On the other hand, the bar does not have to be split into four or eight notes, it could be split in *two,* giving us two **half notes**.

I know it sounds complicated, but it's really just simple math at the end of the day. One bar equals one **whole beat**, two half note beats, four quarter note beats or eight 8th note beats.

Here's a diagram to help you visualize how everything fits together.

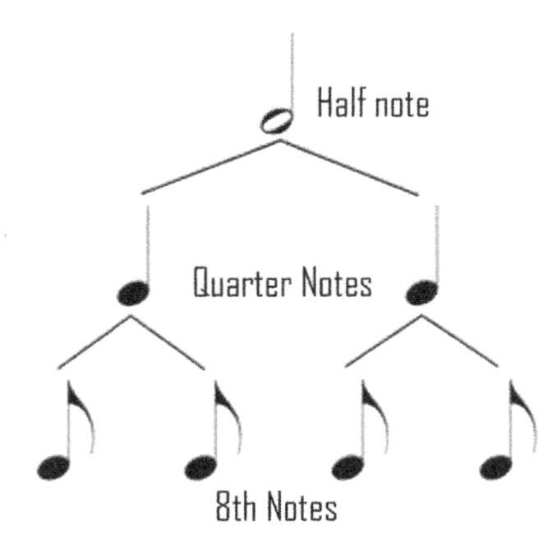

Other Time Signatures

Of course, four isn't the only number of beats that can fill a bar.

It's also common to find three beats in a bar, i.e. 1, 2, 3 — 1, 2, 3. This is represented as 3/4 time—or sometimes referred to as "Waltz Time", because every waltz tune is written in this time signature.

There are many other time signatures as well, but they are more complicated than 3/4 and 4/4, so we're not going to cover them in this book.

So, what does all of this talk about timing have to do with playing guitar? Well, we're going to apply these principles to how we strum notes in the right rhythm.

But first... you should probably learn the proper way to strum:

How to Hold a Pick

How can such power, grit, grunge, beauty, elation and mesmerizing tone come from such a small, seemingly insignificant item?

A guitar pick (or plectrum) may be just a thin piece of triangular plastic — but in the hands of a true virtuoso, kings can be brought to their knees in awe. And part of that power comes from knowing how to hold it the right way.

The pick is held between your thumb and index finger on your strumming hand. It should be parallel to the line of your arm, with the thinner end pointed towards the strings. You should typically hold it as close to the strings as possible.

Here are some useful photos to give you a better idea:

How the pick and your hand should look as you start to strum.

How the pick and your hand should look as you finish strumming.

Bad Technique! The pick is too far to the left.

Perfect Technique! The tip of the pick is lined up to the center.

Bad Technique! The pick is too far to the right.

Holding the pick incorrectly will not only make the guitar harder to play, but you can also develop bad habits that may take a long time for you to break. So, take the time now to develop proper technique now. Make sure it feels comfortable, natural and firm in your fingers before moving on to other techniques discussed in this book.

Strumming

Now that we know some chords, understand basic time signatures, and know how to strum — let's put them all together!

Start with any of the three chords that you've already learned. Play all six strings in just one downstroke (swiping the pick down towards the floor). Now play all six strings with an upstroke (swiping the pick back up towards the ceiling).

This movement is called strumming.

Strumming is an essential skill to master, regardless of the type of guitar you play or the music you want to perform. Here are a few tips to keep you on the right path:

Elbow Not Wrist!

Rest your elbow on the front of the edge of the body of the guitar. Lift your forearm until it lines up with the strings. This is a good starting position.

The strumming motion should come from the elbow — not the wrist.

You want your wrist relaxed, but it should remain straight and in line with your arm at all times. Let your elbow do the work. Your wrist shouldn't be bent in awkward positions or flailing around—then again, you don't want it too stiff where you look like a robot!

In order to keep the strumming even and musical, do your best to keep your upstrokes and downstrokes at the same speed, and apply the same amount of pressure as you play both. You will, of course, change this as you get better and start to play more intricate and dynamic rhythm patterns.

Also, don't make a fist with your strumming hand. Leave the fingers open, which will give you more control. (Even if you're playing angry punk rock — you still don't want to clench a fist!)

Now that we know the basics of the technique, it's time to learn a few rhythms. Here's a very simple one to get started. This is in 3/4 time.

Exercise #34 — Rhythm Pattern 1 — 3/4

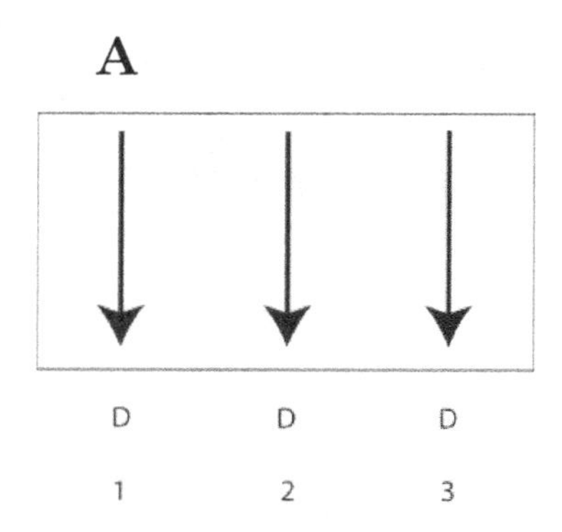

This is a simple one strum per beat rhythm. Count 1, 2, 3 and strum downwards on every beat. "D" signifies a *downstroke.*

> *Check out the audio examples to hear exactly how it should sound.*

Now we'll now add an *upstroke.* This occurs halfway between the second and third downstrokes, which gives us the following pattern.

Exercise #35 — Rhythm Pattern 2 — 3/4

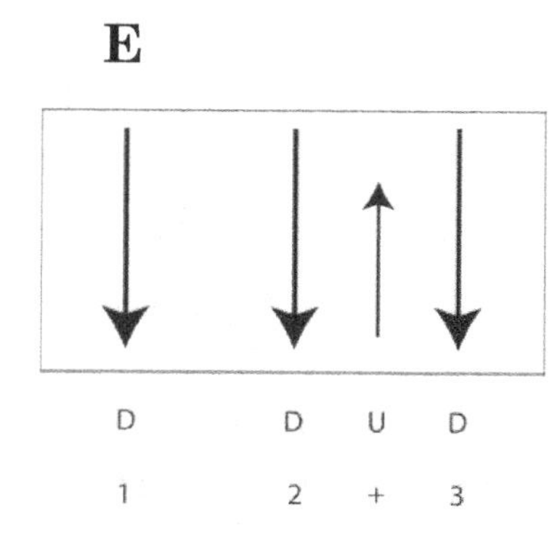

This can either be counted 1, 2&3 or D DUD. Did you notice that by simply adding a single upstroke, we instantly get a far more interesting rhythm that is much more usable within songs?

Now, we'll move on to some more rhythms — but in 4/4 time.

Exercise #36 — Rhythm Pattern 3 — 4/4

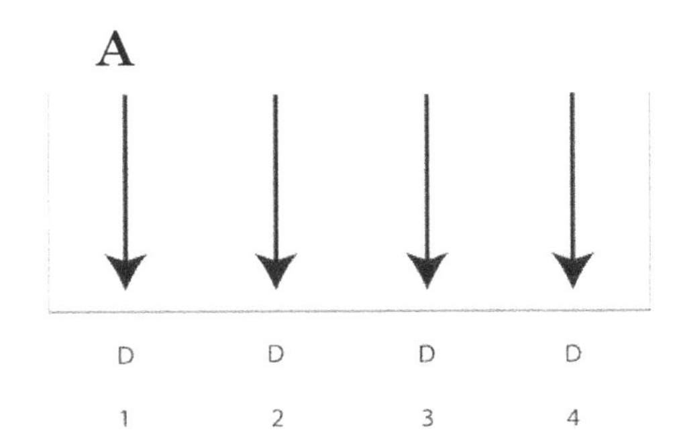

This is a simple one strum per beat rhythm similar to Exercise #34, but this time count 1, 2, 3, 4 and strum downwards on every beat...

> *Listen to the audio example for what it should sound like.*

We'll now add an upstroke as we did for Exercise #35. This one occurs halfway between the third and fourth downstrokes, which gives us:

Exercise #37 — Rhythm Pattern 4 — 4/4

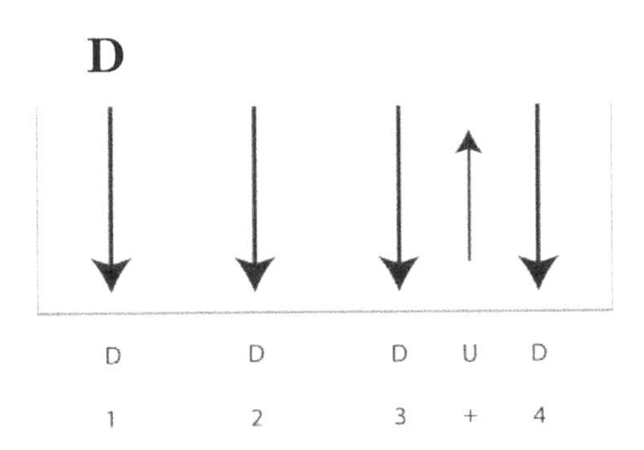

This can be counted as 1, 2, 3&4. Or as D, D, DUD. Again, as with Exercise #35, simply adding a single upstroke gets us a far more interesting sounding rhythm. Refer to the audio example to make sure you're playing it correctly.

Exercise #38 — Rhythm Pattern 5 — 4/4

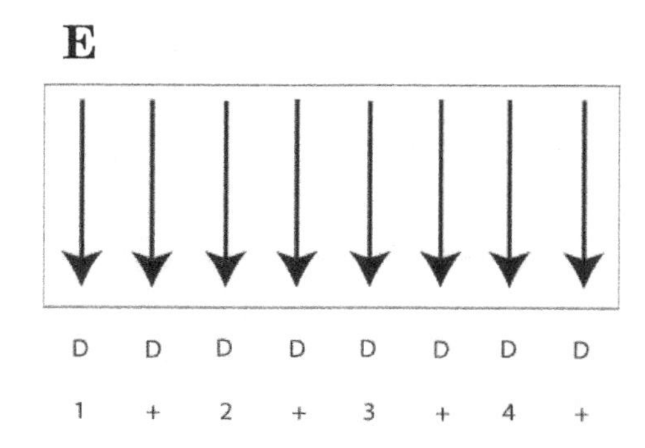

Alright, so now let's play 8 notes instead of 4, as shown in the diagram above. You'll count this as 1&, 2&, 3&, 4&. We'll set the same tempo as before (60-70 BPM), but the strums should occur twice as often. So, there will be TWO strums for every one beat.

Something to keep in mind whenever the tempo and rhythm gets faster is to try and remain as relaxed as possible. Music, as in any art, is a very direct form of self-expression. If you're stressed or anxious, there's a good chance that's going to come across in your playing.

This is why it's important to start slow and be deliberate with every note. You have to gain control first before you can confidently work your way up to faster speeds.

Now that we've got those rhythms down, let's try a few more.

Exercise #39 — Rhythm Pattern 6 — 4/4

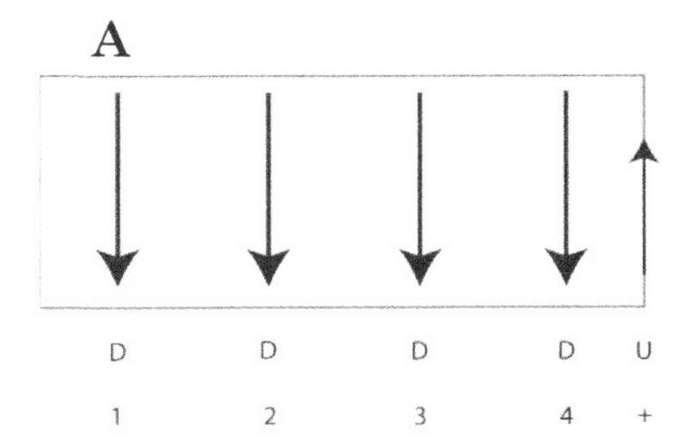

This is similar to the third rhythm pattern we learned but with an additional upstroke played between the last strum of the bar and the first strum of the next bar.

As with all these rhythm patterns, listen to the audio examples to get a feel for what you should be playing and what it should sound like.

Exercise #40 — Rhythm Pattern 7 — 4/4

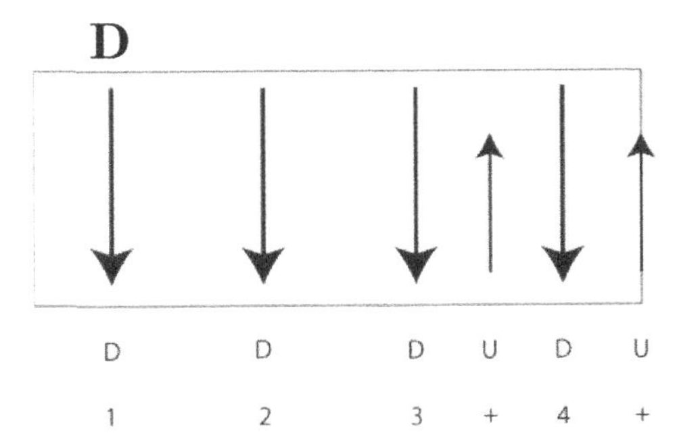

This is a combination of Exercise #37 and Exercise #39.

Exercise #41 — Rhythm Pattern 8 — 4/4

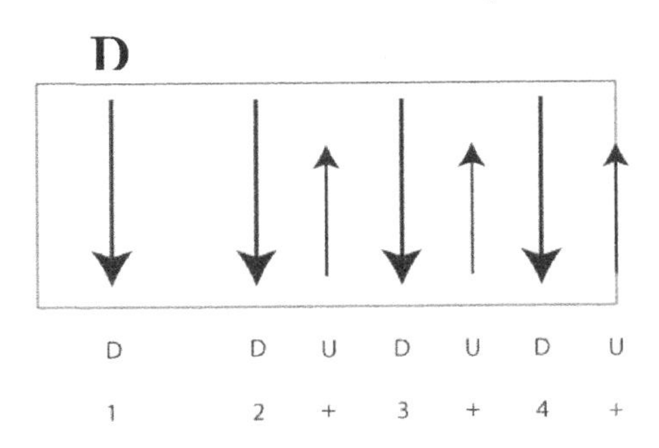

This is very similar to Exercise #40 but with an additional upstroke after the second beat.

Exercise #42 — Rhythm Pattern 9 — 4/4

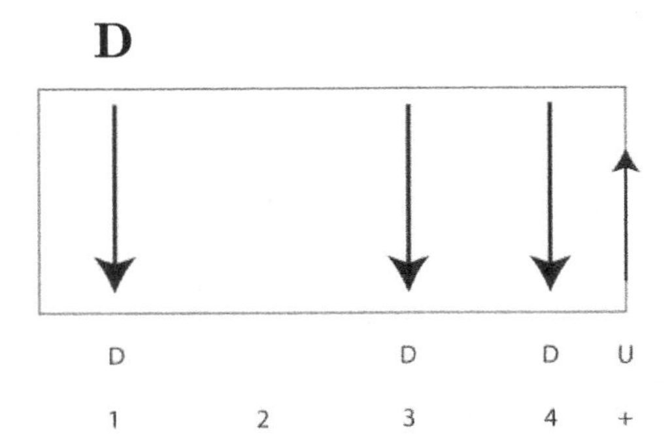

The phrase "less is more" is often associated with music. This exercise therefore includes a **rest,** which gives the rhythm a very different feel to the other ones we've covered so far. (More on "rests" in a bit.)

To play it, strum the downstroke on the first beat, then perform the same motion on the second beat without letting the plectrum touch the strings. Then strum down on the third beat, followed by a down-up strum on the remaining eighth notes that end the bar.

This pattern is used in a lot of slower songs that I'll feature later in the book...

Exercise #43 — Rhythm Pattern 10 — 4/4

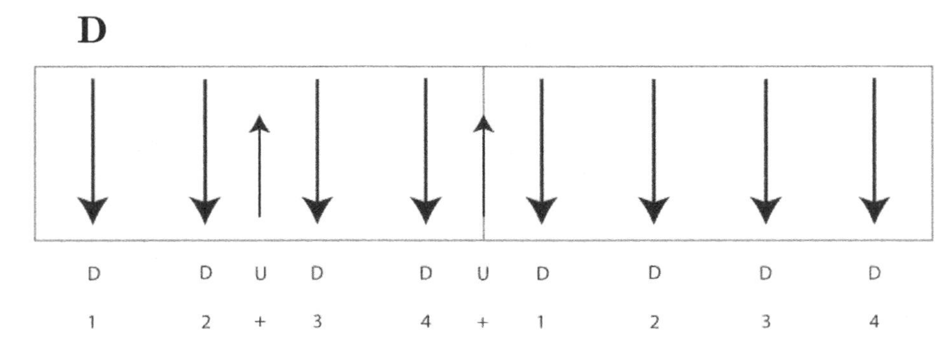

Our final Rhythm Pattern is a two-bar exercise that switches things up in the second half. It's common for strumming patterns to change to reflect what else is happening within the song, like with the lyrics for instance. We'll come back to this pattern later in the book to explain more...

Don't let the first bar throw you with its awkward pattern; play it slowly at first and count the beats out loud as you strum them.

Many guitar teachers often say that "if you can't say a rhythm, you can't play a rhythm." So, if you have trouble with this, forget the guitar and just try and say the rhythm out loud: "Down, Down-up-Down, Down-up-Down, Down Down Down."

You'll be amazed at how much easier your strumming hand falls into place when you connect it with rhythms spoken out loud.

Now let's move on to some Chord Progression Exercises.

Exercise #44 — Chord Progression 1

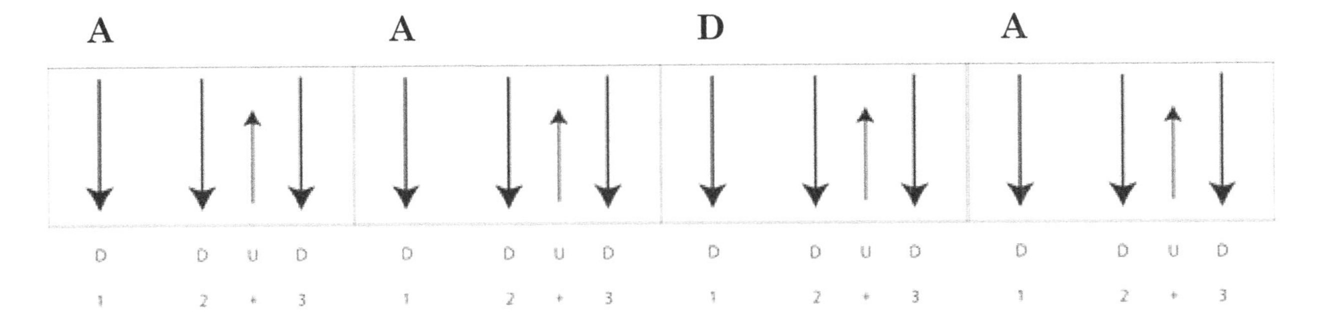

A very simple progression involving only A and D to get you started. Remember the rhythm goes "1, 2&, 3" or "Down, Down-up-Down."

Exercise #45 — Chord Progression 2

> *TIP: The slashes above represent beats of the bar. So, in the above exercise, there are 4 beats in a bar. When you see such slashes — you are free to use any strumming pattern you want.*

Slightly harder this time and involving E, D and A. Again, you can use any of the rhythms mentioned above, but I would still suggest either Rhythm Pattern 2 (Exercise #35) in 3/4 or Rhythm Pattern 4 (Exercise #37) in 4/4 until they become easy to play.

Exercise #46 — Chord Progression 3

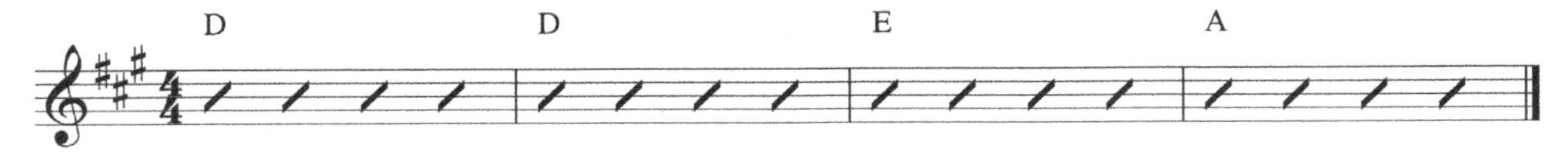

Same chords, different order. Let's try using Rhythm Pattern 6 (Exercise #39) in 4/4 for this one.

And our final two chord progressions for this section are a little longer:

Exercise #47 — Chord Progression 4

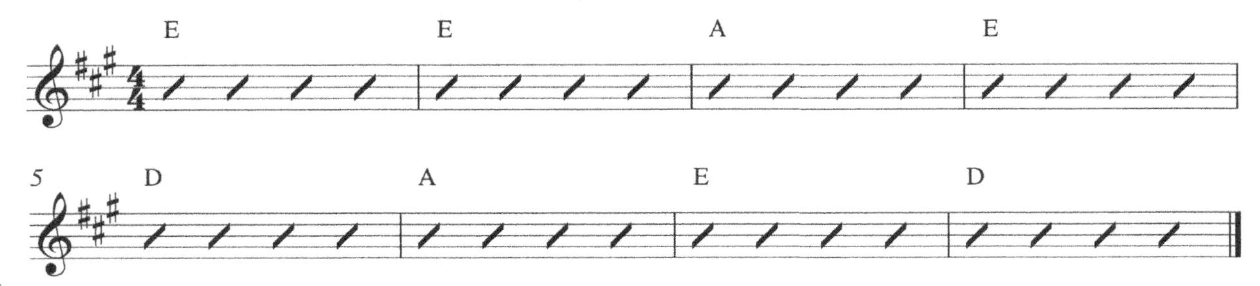

Choose any of the rhythm patterns you fancy having a go at, until they all become second nature.

Exercise #48 — Chord Progression 5

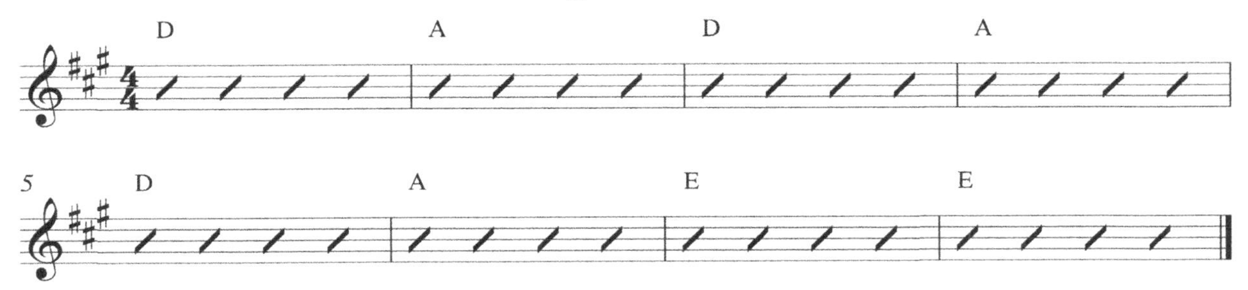

The choice of rhythm pattern is again up to you, just as long as you're switching them up. Don't be biased with any rhythm patterns — otherwise your music will be boring!

Take a Rest...

Well, a musical "rest" that is. The final piece of the rhythm puzzle are the "rests". In music, the silence *between* the notes is just as important as the notes themselves.

In order to stay perfectly in time during these moments of silence, you should still move your strumming arm as you'd normally do to keep the groove going.

Basically, it's as if you were actually strumming, except you're not letting the pick hit the strings. This helps maintain the tempo and a smooth rhythm.

A word of caution here: This will be difficult at first—and you might feel silly doing it—but do it anyway. For beginner guitarists, doing nothing during rests is a surefire way to fall out of the song's rhythm. Don't worry if it feels completely unnatural. Just persevere and remember that a good rhythmic foundation is the key to becoming a good musician.

"As long as you're excited about what you're playing, and as long as it comes from your heart, it's going to be great."

John Frusciante, Red Hot Chili Peppers

CHAPTER 5

Let's Learn Some More Open Chords!

Major Chords

By now you should be well on your way to mastering your first three major chords — A, D, and E. So, let's look at several other open Major chords. These are called C Major (or C) and G Major (or G).

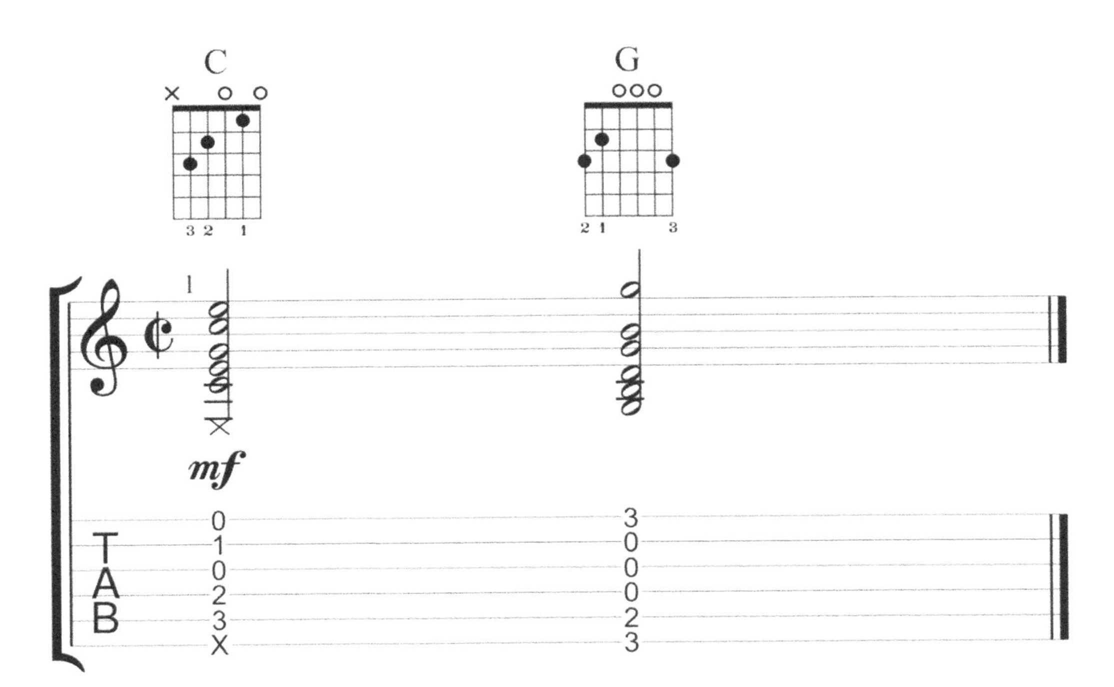

C Major (C)

The most difficult thing about this chord is the spacing between your 3rd finger and 1st finger — it's a bit of a stretch!

G Major (G)

The gap between your 2nd finger and 3rd finger will take some getting used to.

They are slightly harder to play than the first three chords, because they involve more stretching. Remember to follow the steps we outlined when we covered the chords earlier:

First off, just get your fingers used to the position. Play every note of the new chord individually to make sure it sounds good; when they all do, strum it to make sure that all the strings sound great together as well. Then when that's comfortable, strum one of the basic rhythm exercises over the chord and change to a chord you already know well, then change back to the new chord.

Here's some encouraging news: the more chords you learn, the easier and quicker it is to play new ones!

Let's now look at some chord progressions using the chords we already know, as well as the new ones we've just introduced. Choose any of the rhythm patterns we've reviewed for these progressions.

Exercise #49 — Chord Progression 6

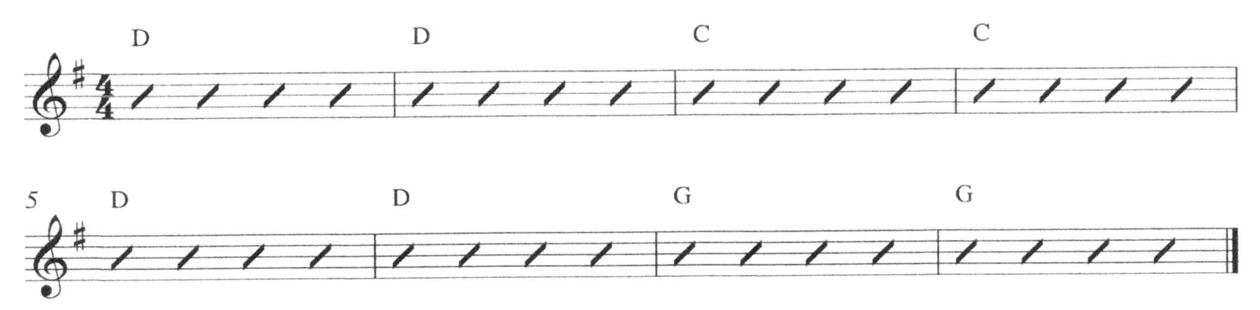

Exercise #50 — Chord Progression 7

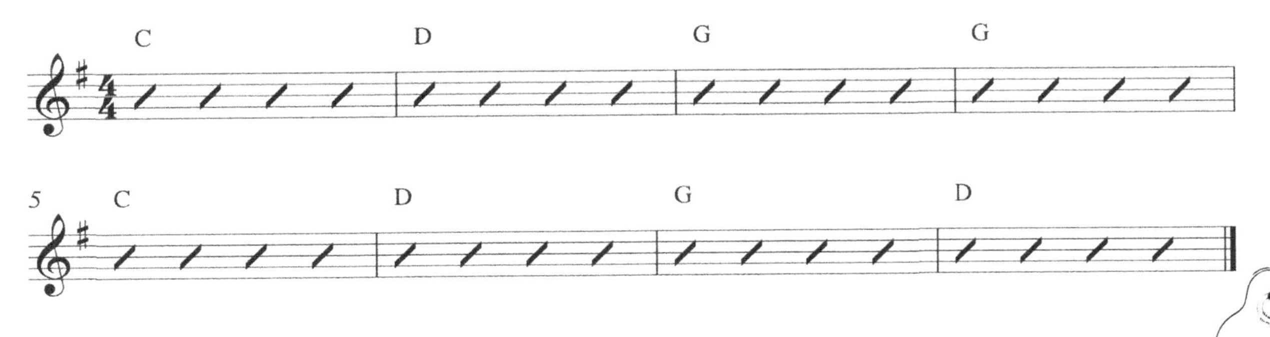

Minor Chords

I mentioned these briefly earlier, but now it's time to learn some Minor chords. You'll notice they have a more melancholic quality to them — perfect for evoking a contemplative feeling in a chord progression!

The three minor chords we will be learning are A minor (or Am), D minor (or Dm) and E minor (or Em).

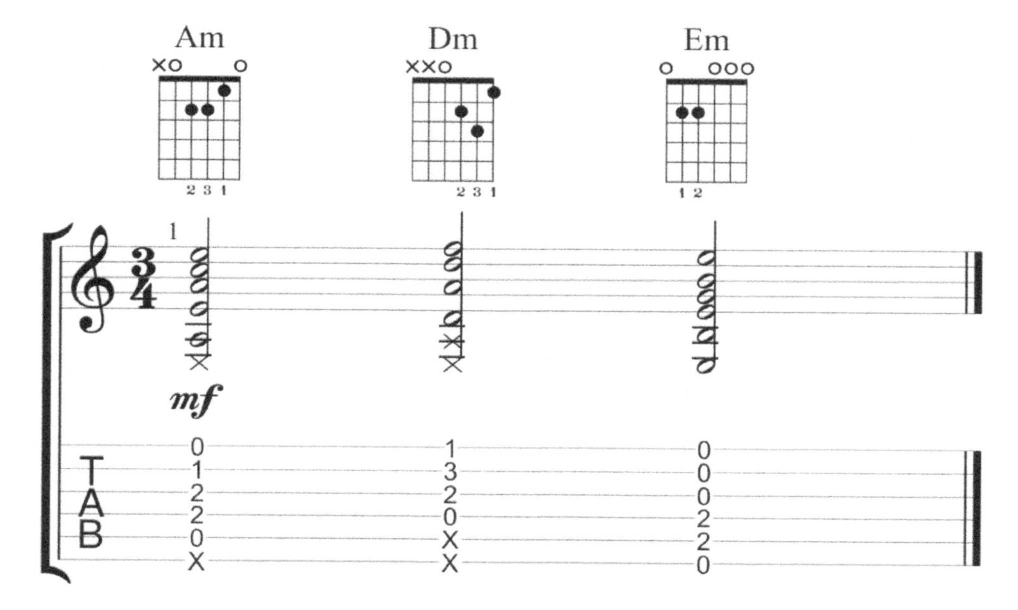

A minor (Am)

You should find A minor very easy to play; it's exactly the same shape as an E major, but every finger is positioned one string over on the fretboard.

E minor (Em)

E minor is even easier! It's an E Major chord without the first finger. You can play it with either your 2nd and 3rd fingers, or you can play it with your 1st and 2nd fingers. There is no right or wrong way; it normally depends on how easy it is to switch from the previous chord or the one you're sliding to.

D minor (Dm)

The last minor chord is D minor, which is played without using the low E or A strings. You therefore start your strum from the D string and continue from there.

This one's a bit harder than the other two minor chords, and it'll take a lot more practice to sound good. It's a wonderful chord, though, and as the legendary Nigel Tuffnel said in the classic movie *This is Spinal Tap*: "It's part of a trilogy, a musical trilogy that I'm doing in D... minor, which I always find is really the saddest of all keys, really, I don't know why. It makes people weep instantly."

And who doesn't want to learn a chord that makes people "weep instantly"?

Exercise #51 — Chord Progression 8

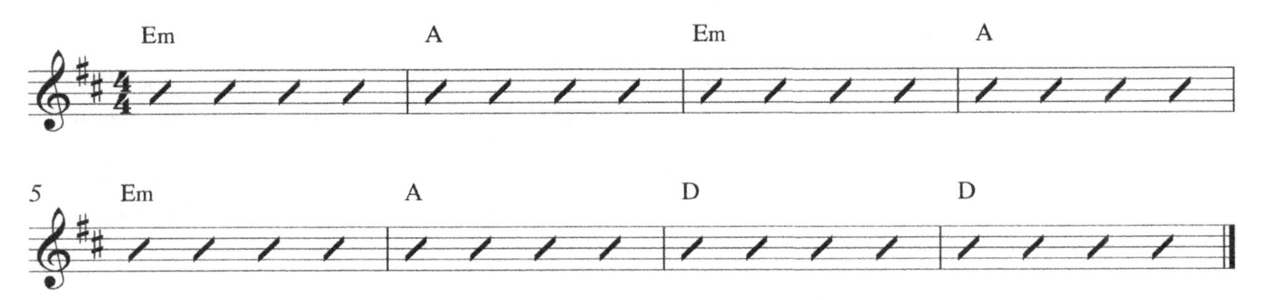

You can make this easier on your hands by using your 1st and 2nd fingers to play the Em, then simply move them down a string and add the 3rd finger to make the A chord shape. Then move them back up without the 3rd finger to reform the Em chord.

The A to D change can be simplified by using the slide technique we discussed in Exercise #32.

Use any Rhythm Pattern you like to play this example.

Exercise #52 — Chord Progression 9

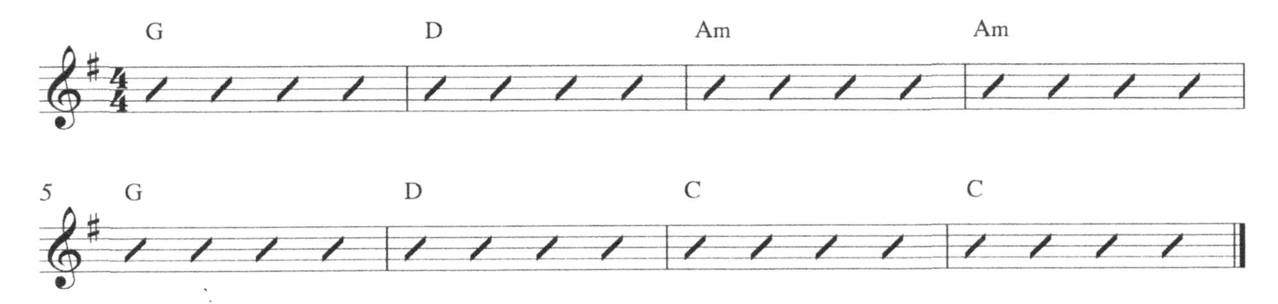

You may well recognize this chord progression; it was used in the classic Bob Dylan song "Knocking on Heaven's Door", which has been covered by numerous bands since then, most notably Guns n' Roses.

Use Rhythm Pattern 9 (Exercise #42) for this one, which is basically the pattern most guitarists use when playing it. It's amazing how good this simple chord progression sounds with a relaxed rhythm pattern.

Exercise #53 — Chord Progression 10

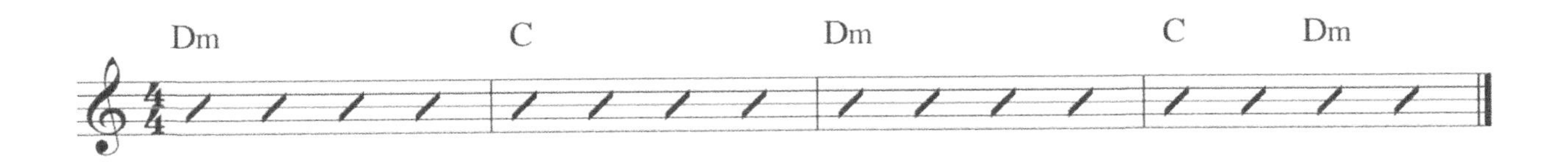

Only two chords, but one of them is the most difficult we've come across so far — the Dm. When you get it down and play this progression quickly, you may be surprised that you're actually playing the folk song "Drunken Sailor".

Start playing it using a simple rhythm, such as Rhythm Pattern 4 (Exercise #37) until you get the hang of the chord changes. Then switch to Rhythm Pattern 10 (Exercise #43) and you'll notice the song come to life...

Here is the pattern again for reference:

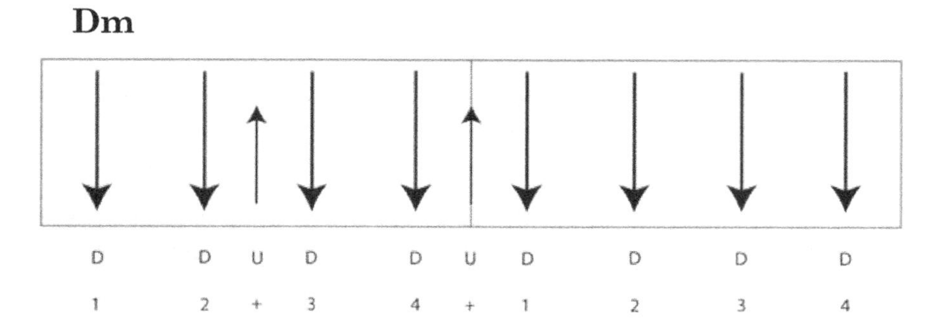

Exercise #54 — Chord Progression 11

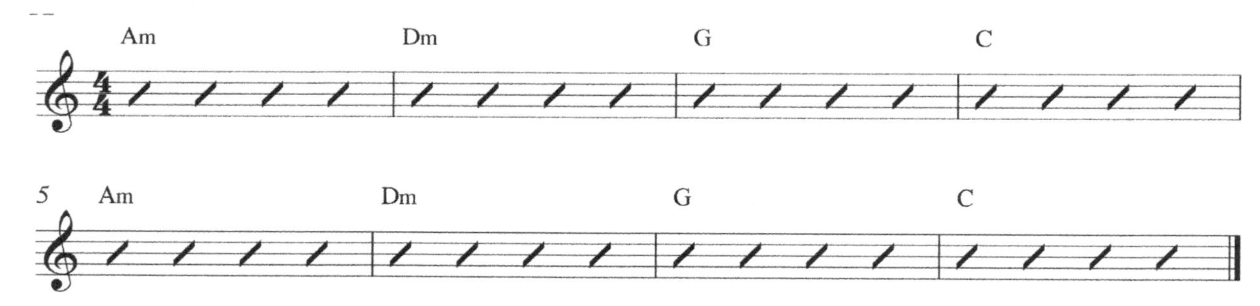

The C to Am change at the end of each fourth bar can be simplified because both chords contain two common fingers. This means that the 1st and 2nd fingers are in exactly the same position for both chords. Changing between them is only a matter of moving the 3rd finger.

This is slightly harder than our first chord progression using a Dm, but you'll find it's actually a simplified version of "Don't Cry" by Guns n' Roses, without the fill at the end and the intricate picking pattern.

Dominant Seventh Chords

These are chords that add character and emphasis to a chord progression or song. It's not necessarily that they sound "happy" or "sad" — they just have a strange sense of feeling unfinished.

The actual musical term is "unresolved"—as if you need to hear another chord after hearing one to "resolve" the slightly odd sound. I don't know. What do they sound like to you?

Dominant Seventh chords are created by adding a minor seventh note to a Major chord.

I can see you scratching your head. I snuck a bit of music theory in there so you become familiar with the terms, but don't worry — you don't need to understand why these chords are what they are at the moment. Just learn how to play them well and make them sound great!

The chords we will be learning are A Dominant Seventh (A7), C Dominant Seventh (C7), D Dominant Seventh (D7), E Dominant Seventh (E7), and G Dominant Seventh (G7).

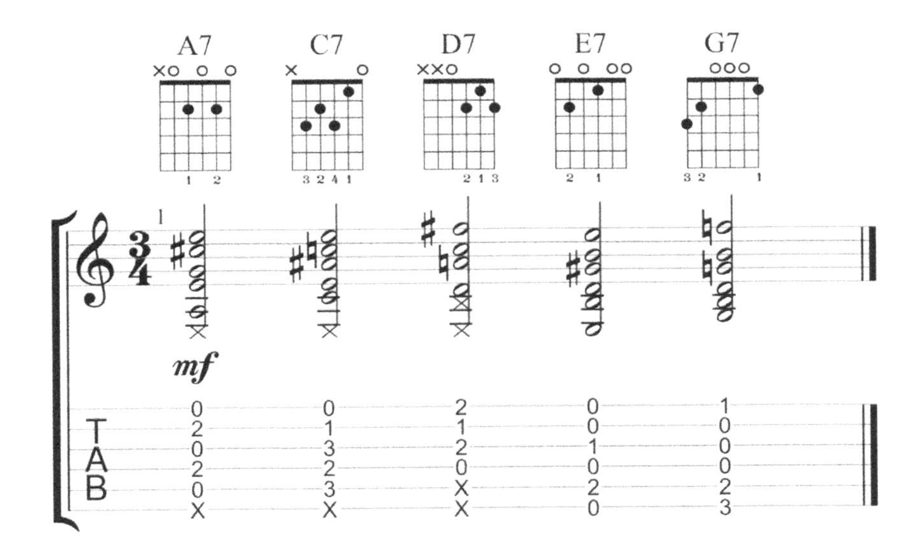

Some of these chords are easy to play. And others... oh boy. The C7 is the first chord you've played so far that uses all four fingers.

Alright, let's go through them one by one...

A Dominant 7th (A7)

This one's easy. It's a normal A Major chord, but without the 2nd or middle finger. It's normally played using the 1st and 3rd fingers; however, like the Em chord, it can be played with the 1st and 2nd fingers (or 2nd and 3rd fingers), if that suits a particular song or chord progression better.

C Dominant 7th (C7)

Even though this uses four fingers, it's actually quite easy after you've mastered the C Major chord. Simply play that C Major chord, then add your 4th finger on the G string on the third fret. But be careful not to touch or dampen the second string (B) when adding the extra finger!

D Dominant 7th (D7)

Again, this is quite easy to play. If you think of the D shape as a triangle, as I do, then a D7 is the same triangle but going in the opposite direction. Therefore, place your 1st finger on the B string on the first fret, your 2nd finger on the G string on the second fret, and your 3rd finger on the high E string on the second fret.

As with all root D chords, try and avoid playing the Low E and A strings; the chords will sound a lot nicer without them.

E Dominant 7th (E7)

This one's a piece of cake. Just like an Em was an E major chord without the 1st finger, an E7 chord is an E Major chord without the 3rd finger.

Didn't I say the more chords you know, the easier it gets!?

G Dominant 7th (G7)

Time to get all stretchy again. 1st finger on the first fret of the high E string, 2nd finger on the second fret of the A string (told you it was a stretch!), and the 3rd finger on the third fret of the low E string (ouch!).

So, there you have them — all the open chords you'll need to play a massive selection of songs. And when you consider how many great songs you could play using only A, D, and E, with all these extra chords the world is truly your oyster.

I would encourage you now to listen with an analytical ear at the subtle differences between Major, minor, and Dominant Seventh chords. Each one evokes a certain feeling or emotion behind the tone, and it'll make you a better musician to understand where and why certain chords are used at particular moments in songs.

As your musical talents grow, you'll be able to point out which chords you're hearing in songs just based on how they "feel" to you. This will of course help you work out songs for yourself by transcribing others' music, or even writing your own tunes.

Exercise #55 — Chord Progression 12

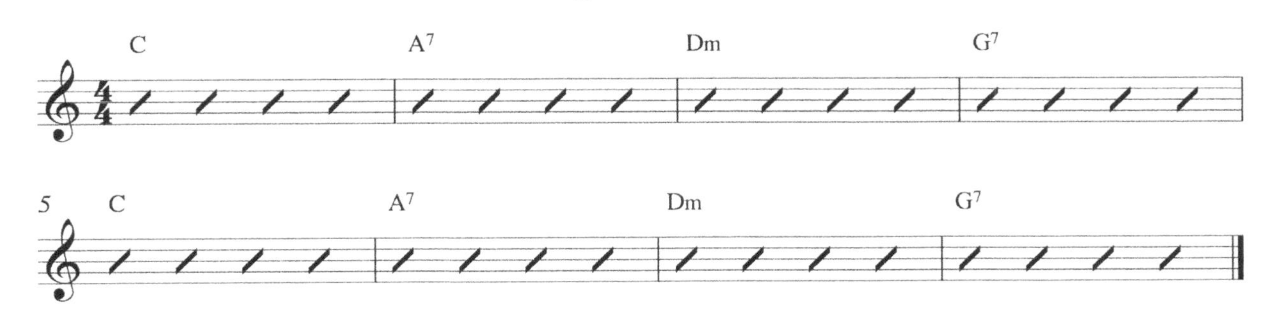

Our first progression using dominant seventh chords uses both the A7 and the G7; it's commonly used in folk songs and even in some pop music.

The Dm to G7 change has one common finger, so you can leave your 1st finger on the fretboard while you change between these two chords.

Exercise #56 — Chord Progression 13

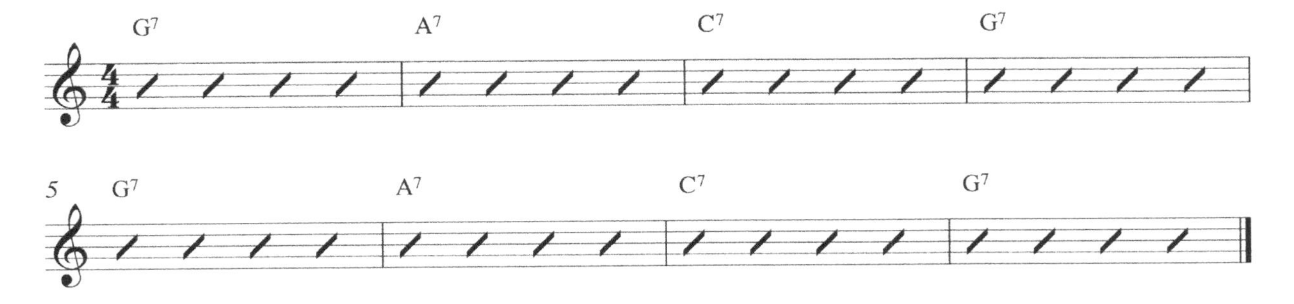

It's unusual to have a song with only dominant chords in it, but those darn geniuses of songwriting, The Beatles, managed it with this chord progression, which is the basis of their song "Sgt. Pepper's Lonely Hearts Club Band".

"The guitarist always looks a bit clever because he's got so many strings and apparently knows what to do with them."

Bernard Sumner, Joy Division, New Order

CHAPTER 6

Let's Scale Things Up

Scales are not a dirty word. They have a reputation of being boring and theoretical, but they are in fact the very heart of music. And when you get the hang of them, you'll be flying around the fretboard and making some seriously sweet tunes!

We're not going to go take a massive dive into theory here, because it isn't necessary at this stage. For now, all you need to know is that a scale is a particular sequence of notes that all sound harmonious together.

They are based around what most of us learn in school as doh, ray, me, fah, so, la, ti, doh.

There are *a lot* of different scales in music. But to keep things nice and simple, we will only be covering Major scales and their relative minor scales in this book.

When practicing any of the following exercises, it's best to play the **root chord** before and after you have played the scale. This will help you visualize how the chord and the scale fit together.

Therefore, to start with play an A chord, then play the scale — both ascending and descending. Then finish off with the A chord again.

So, let's start with the first of the Major scales — A — in its root position:

Exercise #57 — A Major Scale — Root Position, One Octave

Exercise #58 — C Major Scale — Root Position, One Octave

Exercise #59 — D Major Scale — Root Position, One Octave

We're now moving to two octave scales, which involve twice as many notes and are quite a bit harder to play. The following two exercises will involve some finger stretches and moving your hand around the fretboard in order to get them to flow nicely from note to note.

The easiest and most beneficial way to learn and play this exercise is using all four fingers as shown in the diagram below above the notes played. The "0" represents an Open string.

Exercise #60 — E Major Scale — Root Position, Two Octaves

Exercise #61 — G Major Scale — Root Position, Two Octaves

This scale involves using the fourth fret, but there are no notes on the first fret for the three thickest strings (E, A and D), so you can still play the second, third and fourth frets with your 1st, 2nd and 3rd fingers.

Then when you move to the third string (G), move your whole hand to use your first three fingers on the first three frets.

Movable Major Patterns

All the chord exercises that we've covered so far have been in the root position, and they'll come in handy when you want little licks and runs to join chords together in styles such as Blues, Rock, Folk and Country.

Movable patterns are patterns that change depending on where you play them on the neck. We'll stay with the Key of G, as was featured in the last root major scale exercise.

Exercise #62 — G Major Scale — Position 1

The notes in brackets are part of the scale — but you play "through" them, always starting and finishing on the root note. In this case, the G note on the 3rd fret of the low E string.

Exercise #63 — G Major Scale — Position 2

This starts from the same G note on the 3rd fret but moves diagonally up the neck. It's often used for changing position and fast runs when soloing—especially when combined with fragment patterns, which we'll be discussing soon...

I hope you've been doing your Finger Stretch Exercises, because this one does start with quite a reach! Didn't I tell you they'd come in handy? (Pun shamelessly intended.)

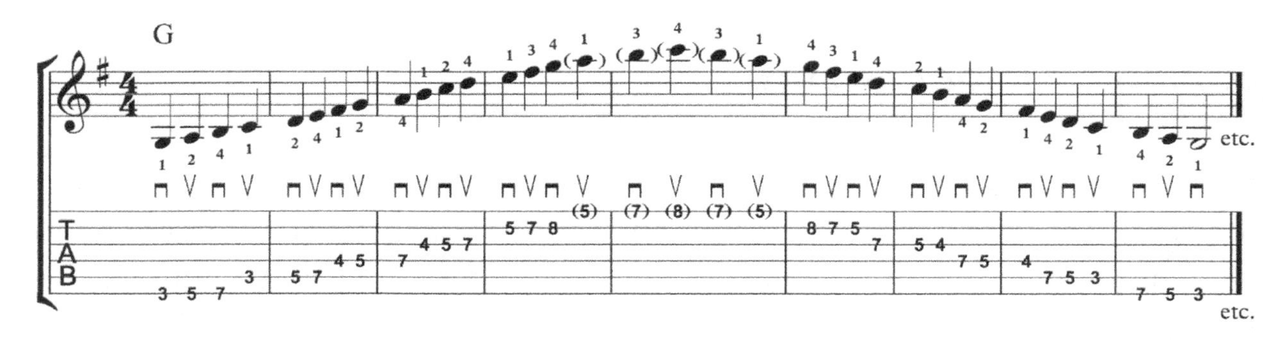

Exercise #64 — G Major Scale — Position 3

Another scale exercise that requires quite a bit of stretching...

Exercise #65 — G Major Scale — Position 4

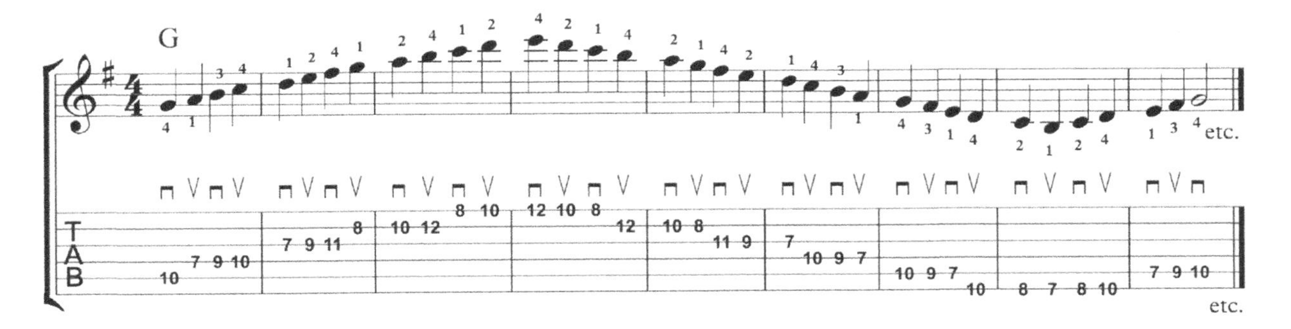

Exercise #66 — G Major Scale — Position 5

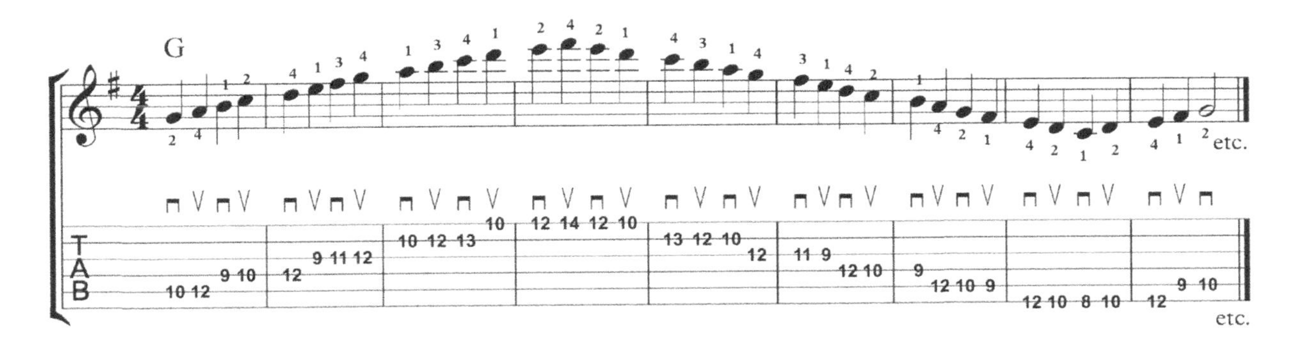

Exercise #67 — G Major Scale — Position 6

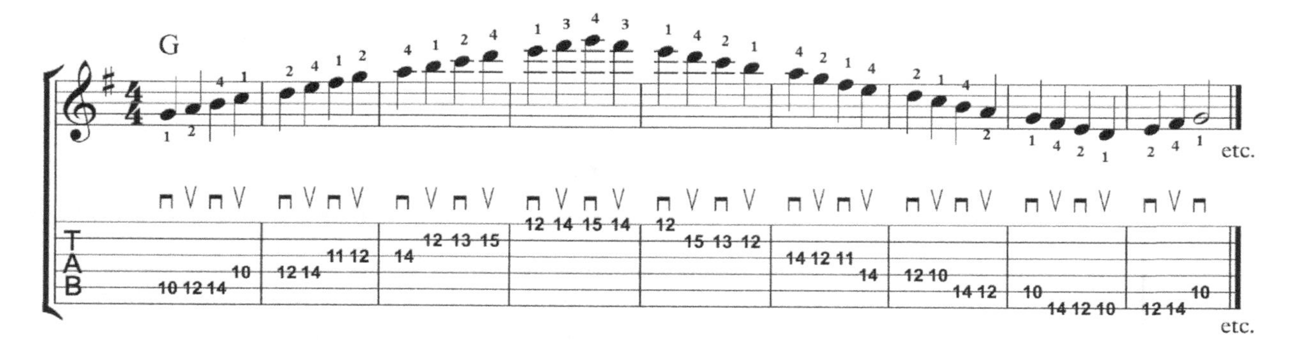

Exercise #68 — G Major Scale — Position 7

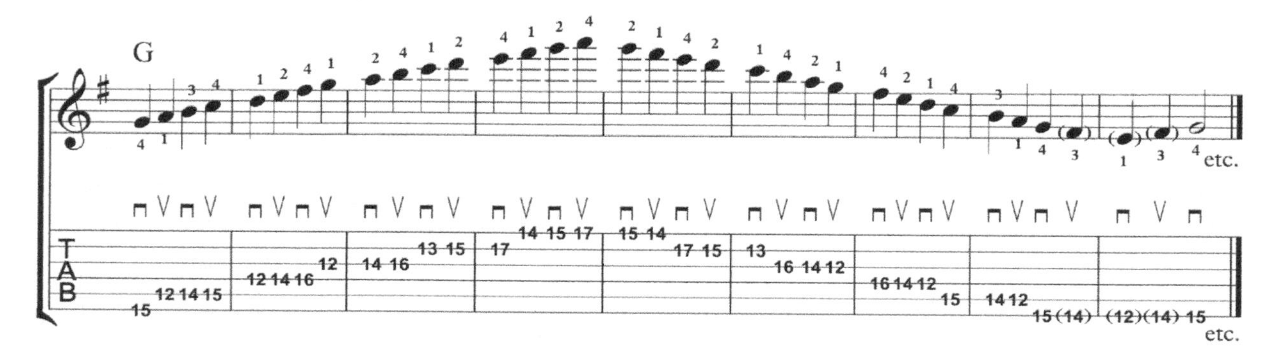

Whew!

We've now covered the seven positions where you can play this scale, from the 1st fret all the way up to the 12th.

But what about the rest of the neck? Well, you just start all over again — but 12 frets higher. For example, the exercise we've just covered can be played again 12 frets higher, with Position 1 starting on the 15th fret as shown below:

Exercise #69 — G Major Scale — Position 1 — Higher Octave

This applies to every other position of the scale as well—so if you want to go higher still, you'd play Position 2 starting at the 15th fret.

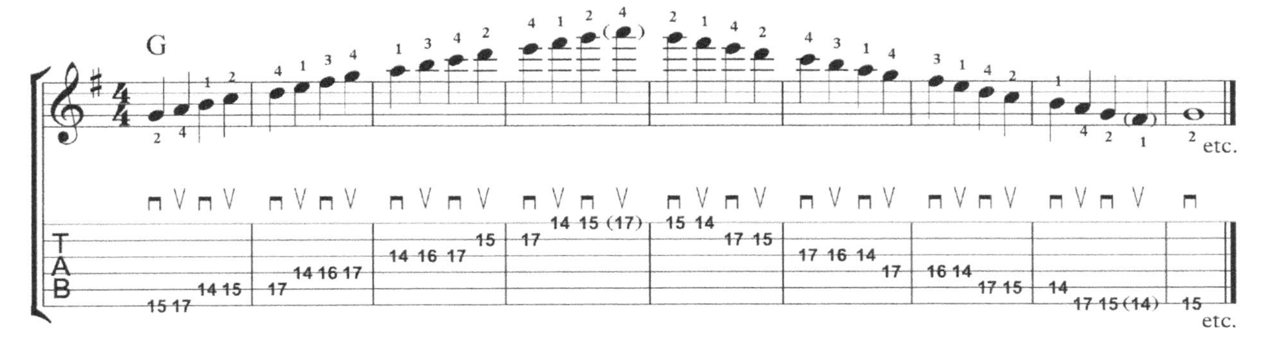

Continuing further, you'd play Position 3 up at the 21st fret. You can now see how you're able to play this scale all over the neck in various positions.

What if you want to play in another Key?

Well, believe it or not, this is very easily done! If you remember, it was important to start and finish the scales on the same note, which in the last six exercises has been the G note in different places across the neck.

In order to play an A Major scale, you would start any of the patterns you've just played — but two frets higher, starting (and finishing) on an A note.

And if you want to play a B Major scale, you just go up two more notes, starting and ending on the B note.

On paper, all these letters and numbers sound overwhelming and confusing. I understand it's a lot to ask of someone just to learn the seven positions we've covered so far. The good news is that, once you memorize them as SHAPES, then it's easy to slide them up or down the neck and play a completely different key.

Therefore, by learning and practicing these seven positions, you will eventually end up being able to play the Major Scale all over the neck in any key you want, over any song there is! Now *that's* exciting—and well worth the effort needed to practice and learn these patterns.

Breaking Them Up: The Magic of Fragment Patterns

Fragment Patterns are the secret to flying around the fretboard at blistering speed—and let's be honest, who doesn't want to be able to do that?

Even if you enjoy playing blues, a slow heartfelt solo can really come to life with a few blazing-fast runs played here and there. Listen to Gary Moore's classic "Still Got the Blues" to hear what I mean.

Fragment Patterns are numerical ways of splitting a scale up into smaller sections, which are then repeated. So, for example, for our first moveable Major pattern (Exercise #62) we can play that again, but this time splitting it up into three note sections, i.e. 1-2-3.

1. We'll start with the first three notes of the scale
2. Then after playing them, we return to the last note we played (the second note of the scale) and play the next three notes up from there.
3. Now we go back one note (to the third note of the scale) and then play three notes up from there.
4. This pattern is then repeated until we have completed the scale.

Sounds complicated—and it is at first—but when you get your head around it, it gets much easier. Plus it makes learning the scales, their shapes, and how they relate to each other much more intuitive.

Here, let me show you…

Exercise #70 — G Major Scale Fragment Pattern 1 — 1-2-3

I've deliberately spaced this exercise out to show what is happening with the notes. After you understand the concept, play it perfectly in time to a metronome with the speed increasing at the usual rate. As always, use alternate picking and make sure that every note rings clear.

You'll notice that I've also introduced **triplets,** these which are sets of three notes that are played together.

You can see that we're in 4/4 time, with four sets of triplets in each bar. This means that each triplet, or group of three notes, occupies the space of one beat. So, when counting them out, instead of saying "1, 2, 3," we would count "tri-p-let, tri-p-let, tri-p-let" to the same beat. This creates a different feel to playing even numbers of notes on every beat and is a useful technique to develop for adding variety and interest to music.

Refer bonus material for audio reference.

Exercise #71 — G Major Scale Fragment Pattern 1 Reverse — 3-2-1

Once you've got the hang of the previous exercise, you can try playing it in reverse.

Now that we've covered both directions, let's join these exercises together and play the scale both up and down using the 1-2-3 and 3-2-1 fragment patterns.

This fragment pattern can obviously be used with any scale, so try playing it over the second position G Major scale, then the third, until you can play it easily in all seven positions.

Now let's play the whole thing backwards!

Exercise #72 — G Major Scale Fragment Pattern 2 — 3-2-1 / 1-2-3

Basically, the same as Exercise #70 and #71 combined, but you reverse the order.

This is quite a bit harder than the previous two exercises, and it may take a while to get your head around it. But think back to the Stevie Vai mind frame I discussed earlier: If you practice things that are far harder than you'll ever play in a real song, then that will make your performances that much easier.

This, like all the others, can be played over any of the positions of the Major or any other scale. And it can be taken even further, such as 1-3-2, 2-3-1; 1-3-2, 2-3-1, etc.

Now, let's try doing it with four notes!

Exercise #73 — G Major Scale Fragment Pattern 3 — 1-2-3-4 / 4-3-2-1

Are four notes better than three? Well, it depends –but with this exercise, they'll certainly stretch the ability of your brain and fingers to work together. That's a good thing, right?

... Right?

As with all these exercises, start slowly until you get your head around the concept. Then when you can play it reasonably well, introduce a metronome at a medium speed and play to that.

Fragment patterns can be played in endless ways; it's up to your imagination and your patience as to how far you push them. They can be played with any number of fingers, in any order, ascending or descending over any position of any scale in any key. So, the options really are limitless!

My advice is to master the easier ones, then move on to something a little harder in whatever way you fancy—more notes, more complicated sequence, more complicated scale, etc. Just don't keep on practicing the same old ones. Be sure to vary them—it's much more beneficial to your development, and it'll make practice far less tedious.

Full disclosure: As these patterns get harder, they should really be classified as advanced exercises. I realize they're a bit of a stretch for beginner players—and I'm not trying to pull a fast one on you, I promise! I just want you to see the concept behind them. I hope you'll realize that, as you improve as a guitarist, fragment patterns will always be a part of your practice and warm up routines. Basically, the better you get, the harder you can make them!

OK, let's switch gears for a minute. I want to talk to you about some other playing techniques.

Hammer-ons, Pull-offs and Slides

Articulation refers to how a player can apply subtle technique to a note in order to color the sound, affect the dynamics, or create a slight variety to the music.

The three most common forms of articulation for playing guitar are **hammer-ons**, **pull-offs** and **slides**.

Hammer-ons

Don't you love it when a musical term actually describes what it is?! Here's a great example of that. Hammer-ons involve you "hammer"ing your finger "on" to the fretboard. Told you it was descriptive!

Well, it's not quite like knocking a three-inch nail into your fretboard... but let me explain. When you hammer a note on the guitar, your finger must strike with enough strength so that the string rings out and sustains. You're basically pounding the tip of your finger onto the string to sound the note.

It differs from a normal plucked note, in that you're actually not playing the note with your pick—you're creating the effect from your fretting hand. You'll hear the difference once you actually try it. So, go ahead — pluck an open string or note as normal, and then "hammer" your finger onto the already-resonating string and see what happens.

As always, the best way to practice any new technique is with an exercise, so here's the first position A Major scale played using hammers from the first finger. It's exactly the same shape as the G Major scale we've just been practicing, only positioned two notes higher up the fretboard starting on the A note on the 5th fret of the E string.

Exercise #74 — A Major Scale 1st Position Hammer-On Exercise

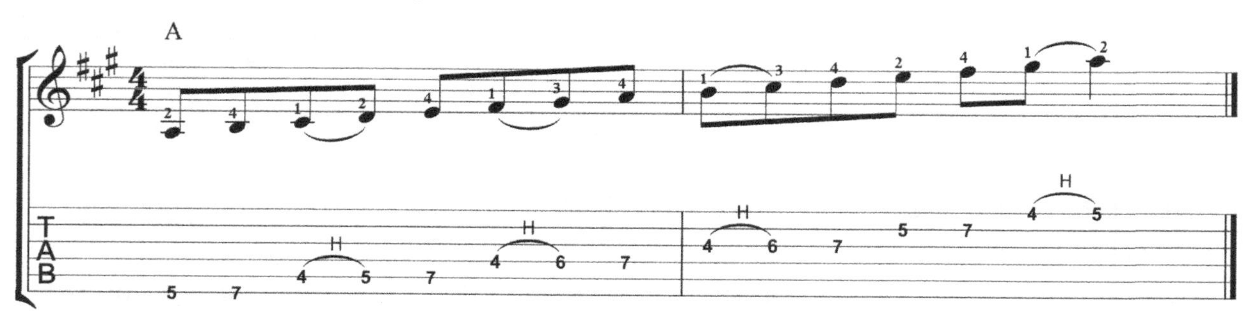

Play the first and second notes of the scale as you normally would, then play the third note (the C# on the A string). For the next note—while your 1st finger is still on the C# and the string is still resonating! —you're going to "hammer" your 2nd finger onto the next note of the scale — the D. The next note (E) is then played as normal.

On the next string down (the D string), play the first note (F#) and then hammer into the sixth fret with your 3rd finger, creating the next note of the scale — G. This is followed by a G#, which is played normally.

This technique continues until you finish the scale.

Pull-Offs

We'll now move on to pull-offs, which are fundamentally the opposite of a hammer-on, in that you pull off a note to get another note. However, it's a bit more than just raising your finger, because that in itself wouldn't produce a very loud and clear note. You actually have to pick the string with your fingertip to get the note to sound fully.

This takes a little practice, and it's best done with a downward motion of your fret-hand finger. Be careful not to pick the string below the note you're pulling off from.

Exercise #75 — A Major Scale 1st Position Pull-Off Exercise

This is basically the same exercise as above, but you're pulling off instead of hammering on. We're going to start from the highest note of the scale and then move backwards.

Exercise #76 — Combining Hammer-ons and Pull-offs

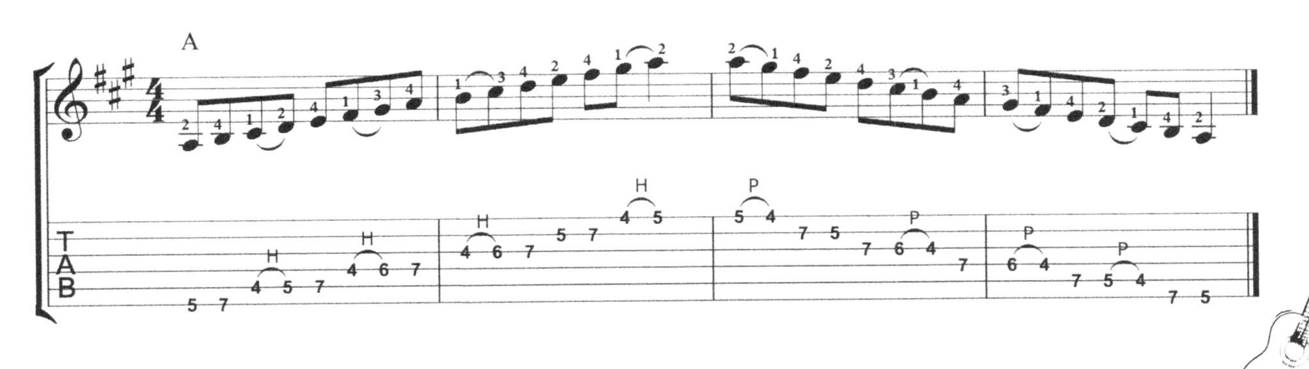

Now let's join the two exercises together! You'll hammer on going up the scale, and then pull off coming down.

Exercise #77 — Hammering with the Little Finger

That little pinky of yours is obviously your weakest finger, so using it for hammer-ons in the early stages won't exactly produce the greatest results. So, let's whip it into shape!

This exercise is designed to build strength into your pinky, which will prove ever so useful for many songs--and especially solos that you'll end up playing in the future.

Let's mix things up by playing this on the 7th fret in B Major.

Exercise #78 — Pull-offs with the Little Finger

Pinky still has some strength left? Let's do the same scale backwards, using pull-offs with your little finger.

Remember that you can play these exercises using any finger combination over any scale. Change them up to different positions and different keys, so that things don't get stale or you become stuck in one position on the fretboard.

Exercise #79 — Further Up the Neck Combination

Moving up the neck, we'll do a hammer-up and pull-off run using the first and corresponding finger for this fourth position C Major scale.

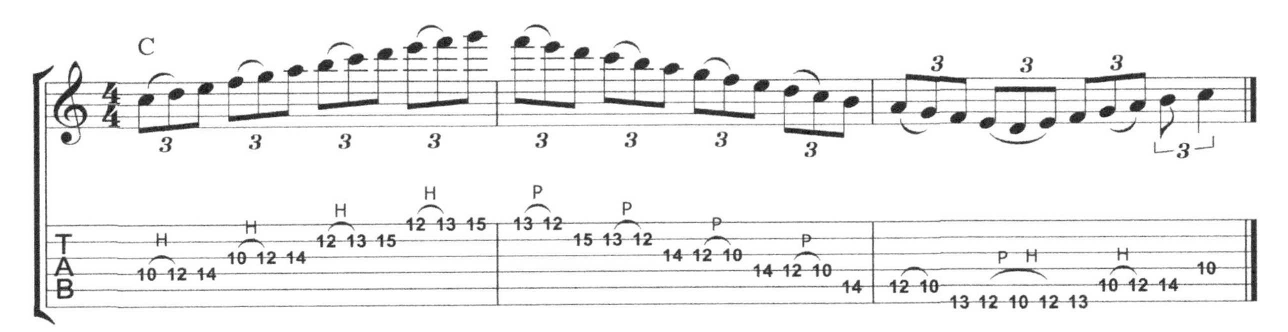

Exercise #80 — Taking It Further — Three Note Hammer-ons and Pull-offs

Maybe you've guessed, but you are not restricted to hammering only one finger; you can actually hammer two, creating three notes from a single strike with the pick!

This is understandably quite a bit harder to do, because not only does it require more strength than any of the previous exercises, but also a lot more accuracy.

Fair warning: This is an advanced technique. But the sooner you start practicing it, the sooner you'll amass thousands of raving fans.

We'll do this one in the Key of D for variety. We'll stick with the first position scale, though, because it's the one you're probably most familiar with at this stage. As with the rest of the exercises, this would work with any scale in any key.

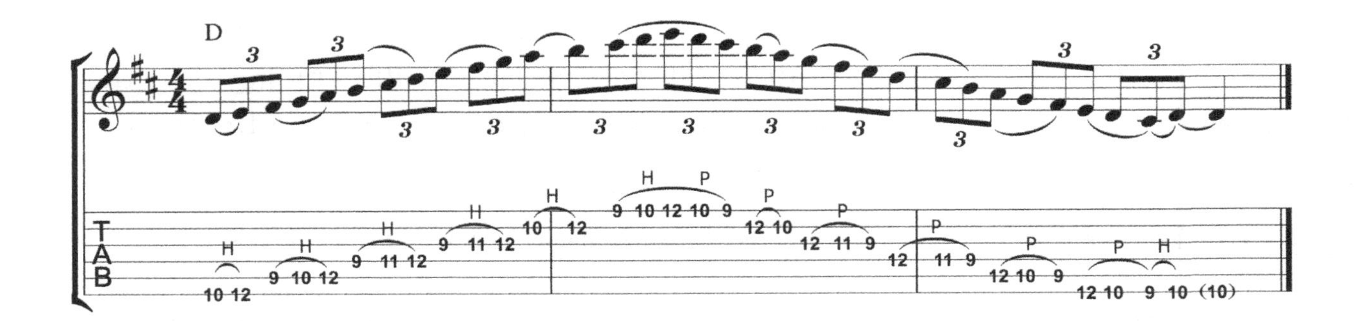

Slide Away

Sliding, as the term implies, involves sliding a finger up or down the neck, allowing you to pluck one note but hear two (or more) — plus you get this really killer sliding sound in-between them.

Slides are often used in licks and solos, but they're also a superb way to move between different scale patterns. You therefore start to play "across" the neck, as opposed to simply up and down it.

The basis of learning to play this way is that there are two simple rules:

1. You can either slide a finger within a scale position on a note that is shared in both scales. This is most useful for three note per string scales, such as Major Scales.

2. Or you can slide any shared note that is played by the same finger between two scale patterns. This is most useful for two note per string scales, such as Pentatonic or Blues Scales.

This is really just a matter of working out what notes can and can't be used to slide.

Let me explain...

The easiest example of this is moving between the first and second positions of a G Major Scale by sliding a note on the D string.

First, play the first five notes of the first position G Major scale as normal. Then, when you get to the sixth note (E on the D string), rather than playing the following note (F# on the D string) with your 3rd finger, you'll instead slide your 1st finger up to that note.

You then continue playing the rest of the scale in the second position. Once you reach the final note, come back down to the cross-over point--but this time slide your 1st finger back from the fourth to the second fret on the D string, and then finish off the scale back in the first position.

This is shown in the following exercise:

Exercise #81 — G Major — D String Slide Between First and Second Positions

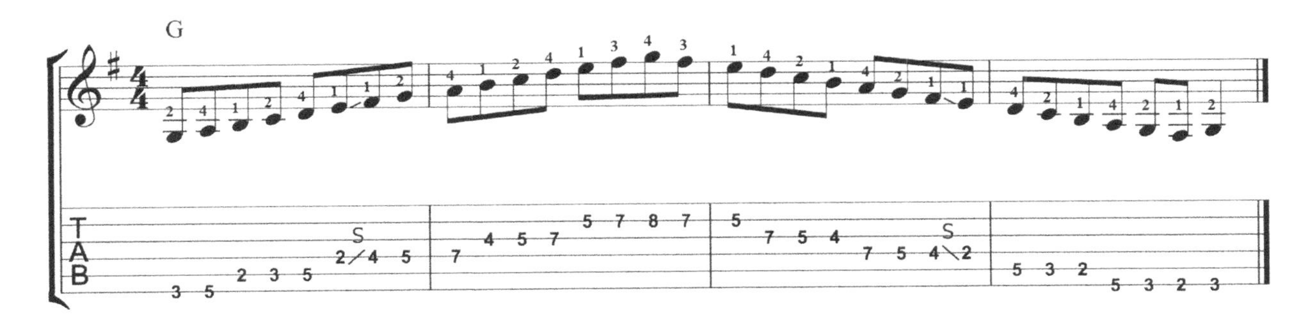

This example shows the first slide method, which is sliding within the same scale position to bridge the note that allows you to slide between both the first and second positions.

Obviously, there are many other places within the scale that the same technique could be used. For example, it also works if you slide on the A string –but this is quite a stretch, so we'll do it on the G string.

Exercise #82 — G Major — G String Slide Between First and Second Positions

This is very similar to the above exercise, and the slide takes place in the same position using the same fingers — but on the G string.

More Major Scale Variations

Now that you understand the basic concept, you can find places to slide between the other scale position pairs — 2 to 3, 3 to 4, etc.

Don't limit yourself to just changes between consecutive positions! You can get really daring and slide between the first position and the third position of the scale, or even the fourth or fifth or whatever! Just keep expanding your knowledge and you'll end up sliding around the neck like a duck on a frozen lake.

Easier Options

Let's now briefly cover the other option, which is sliding a common note within two different scale positions. This is particularly useful with Pentatonic scales, Blues scales, and other simplistic scales.

However, it cannot be used with Major scales, or other three notes per string scales, because of the increased complexity.

Now that you know how it all works, have a go at changing between the first and second positions of any Pentatonic scale by sliding a finger on a common note from the first position to the second. There are lots of options. With some of the positions you can slide with either finger and still keep the scale going without losing position. Fantastic fun!

In the words of Oasis frontman, Liam Gallagher: "Slide away!"

Staccato and Legato

In our continued discussion of articulation, let's have a chat about what staccato and legato mean. I'm pretty sure you've heard the term staccato; it's commonly used in everyday English to describe anything that is choppy or broken up. Legato is the opposite; it means something that is smooth and seamless.

All the scalar exercises that we've covered in this book should have been played as legato as possible, with every note flowing seamlessly into the other. But if all we did was ever play legato then our music would be pretty boring. Variety is the spice of life—so sometimes we want to play staccato.

And this involves muting.

Two methods...

There are two basic ways to mute a note: either with your strumming hand or with the fingertips of the fretting hand.

For this book we'll only be covering strumming hand mutes, which can either be done by palm muting or full hand muting, as is used in Flamenco and other similar styles of playing.

Palm Muting involves laying the edge of your palm (not the palm itself), from the end of your little finger to your wrist, very gently on the strings right at the base of the bridge on your guitar. Your palm will face towards the headstock so that you can still strum or pick the strings.

And by "very gently" I mean just that. If you press too hard, you'll just hear a thud — not a nicely dampened note. (This "thud" does have its place if you want a percussive sound from your guitar, but it's what we're going for here.)

The type of guitar you're playing, and even the type of bridge you have, will also affect how you perform this technique. Experienced players mute differently depending on what guitar they are playing.

Become a Muting Master

The simplest way to master palm muting is to place the edge of your hand on the bridge without touching any of the strings, then start strumming downstrokes without moving your hand from its position. You will obviously have restricted hand movement and won't be able to do long sweeping strums, but these kinds of motions aren't needed for palm muting anyway.

Once that gets comfortable, move your hand ever-so-slowly, millimeter by millimeter onto the strings, gently strumming as you go. As you move the edge of your hand, you will begin to hear the strings dampen in sound, though they will still maintain their clarity.

As you move your hand further, the tone will change and become more dampened, until you end up with the "thud" I described earlier. When that happens, move your hand back to the position where the notes are dampened but still sound clear. If you go too far back, they will sound "normal" or "open" again—so change direction until you get the desired sound.

The more staccato you want the notes to sound, the further from the bridge you play. But we're honestly talking a miniscule amount here, like millimeters. And as with everything on the guitar, the more relaxed and comfortable you are, the better this will sound.

Might take a while...

It's going to take some practice until you're at a place where you can quickly find this ideal spot at the drop of a hat when playing songs. But working this into your 10-minute daily practice sessions is well worth the effort.

Palm muting can give you this incredibly awesome sound, especially when used with massive distortion in heavy rock, punk, thrash, hardcore, industrial, etc. But it's often found in anything from pop to R&B using cleaner guitar tones.

It's a widely used technique, and one that you'll most definitely end up using at some point.

Try practicing it with any of the exercises I've laid out for you in this book. Experiment with it. Make Metallica proud!

> *"Although I'm a lead guitarist, I'd say that a good 95 percent of my time onstage is spent playing rhythm."*
>
> *Kirk Hammett, Metallica*

CHAPTER 7

More Advanced Chords

I think that's quite enough scales for a while. So, let's return to chords—but we're gonna step up our game with some more advanced ones. And these are the Maj7th and the Min7th.

Best to cover the root positions first..:

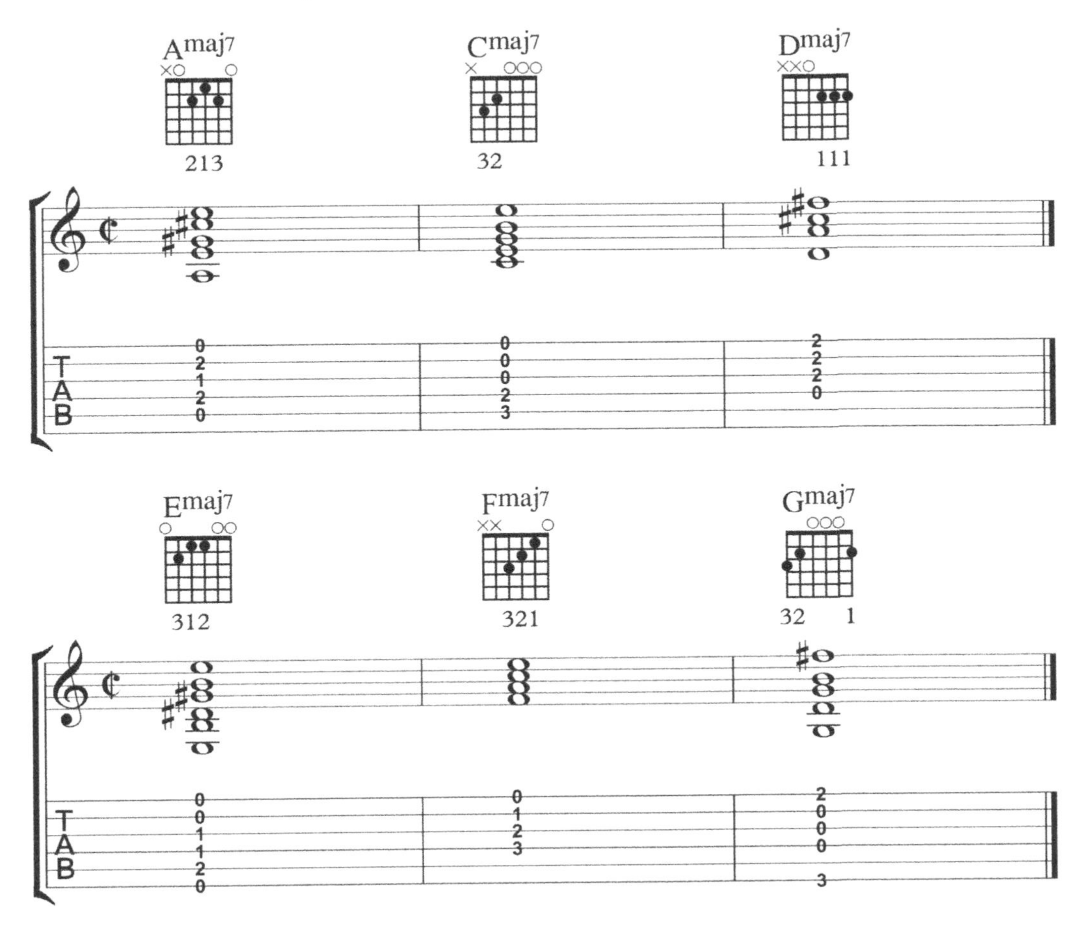

None of these chord shapes should cause you any issues—especially if you've already been practicing with the previous chords we've covered.

Here's what they look like for visual reference:

Amaj7

Cmaj7

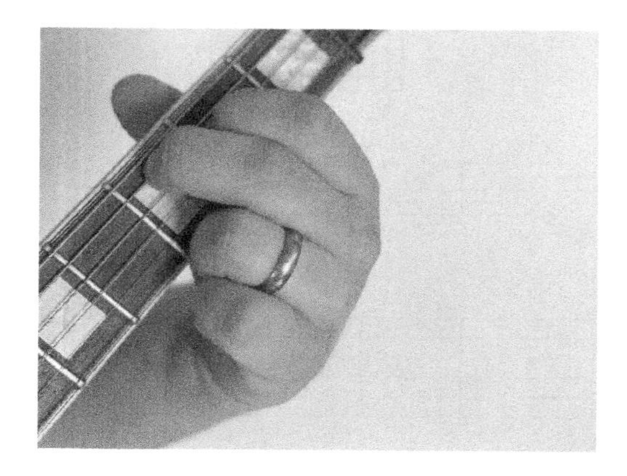

Dmaj7

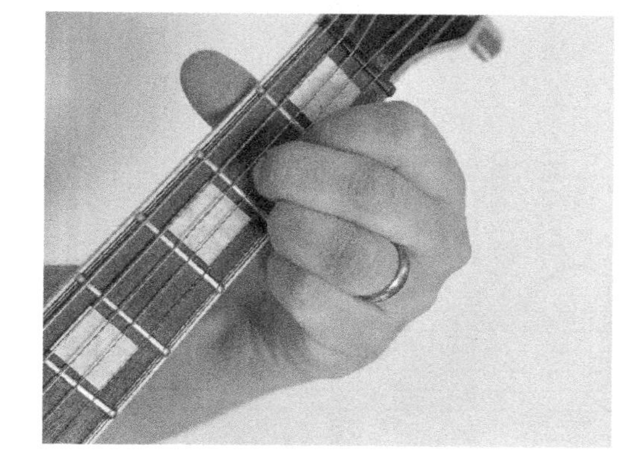

Emaj7

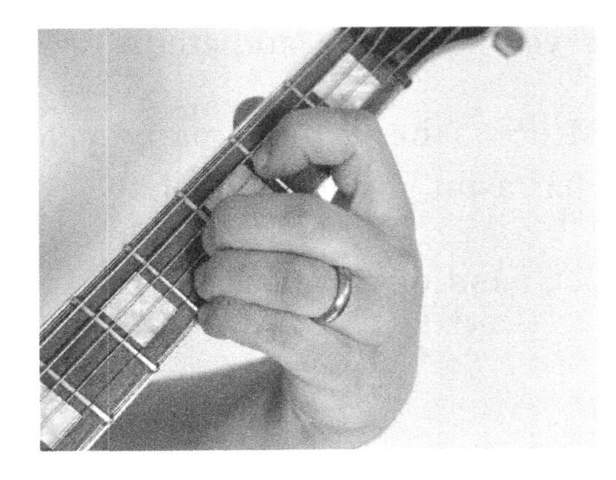

Fmaj7

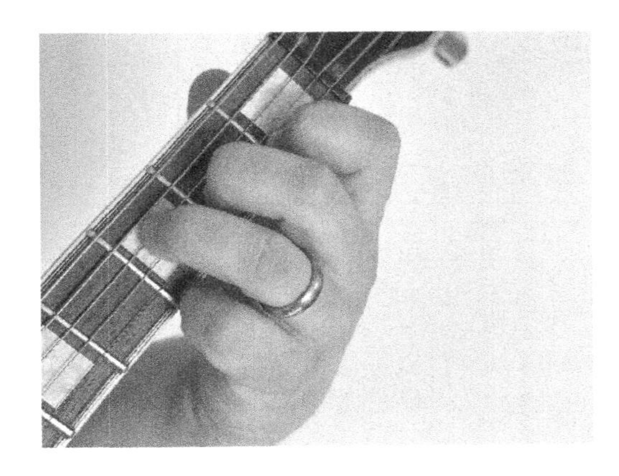

Gmaj7

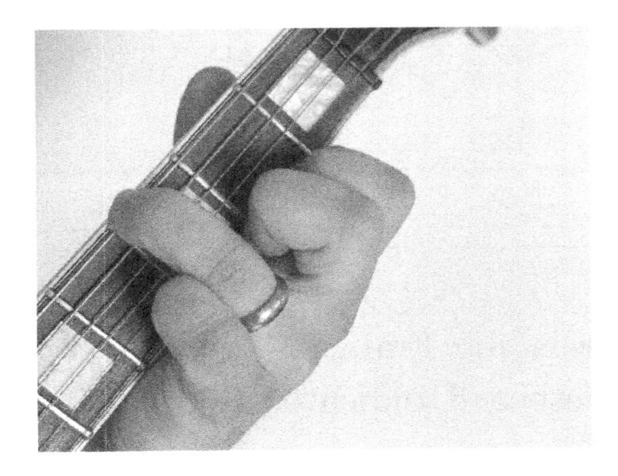

The Sound of the 7th

Major 7th chords have a distinctive sound that is sweet and mysterious. To most people they sound dreamy or jazzy. But we all hear chords differently, so I suggest you play them all through and discern for yourself what they sound like. I guarantee you'll become addicted!

The same is true of Minor 7ths, which many people describe as again being dreamy — but with a bit more melancholy.

Let's go through the root positions of those...

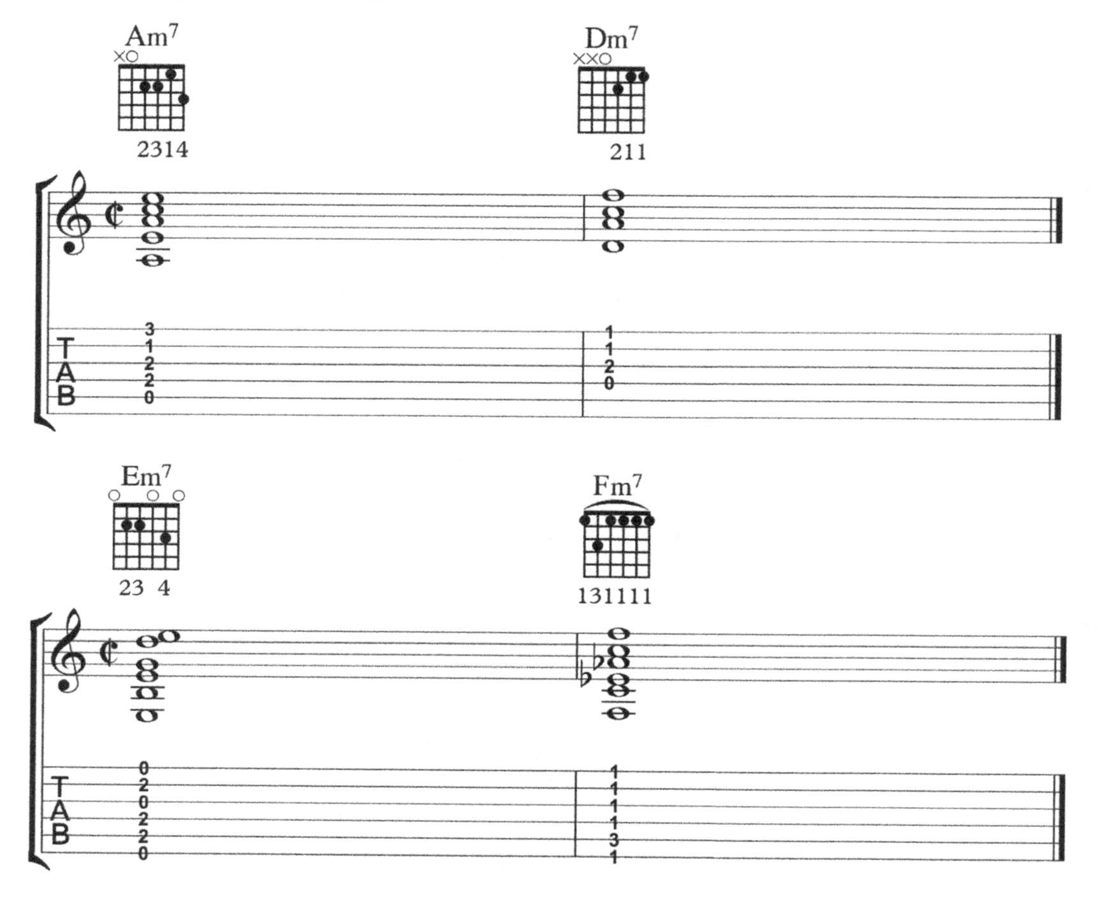

The only surprise here is the Fmin7 — your first barre chord. That line that arcs across the fretboard indicates that all those notes are "barred" with your finger.

To play this particular chord, lay your index finger flat across the entire fretboard at the 1st fret. For the best sound, and to avoid muddiness or accidental muting, use the edge of your finger where the bone is.

Not gonna lie... barre chords are tough—and they'll require some serious strength and stamina for them to sound perfectly. Pay close attention to the photo below for a better reference of how your finger should be positioned.

Amin7

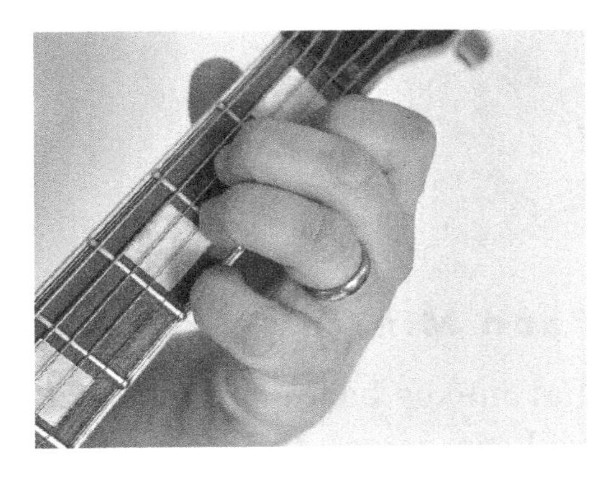

Dmin7

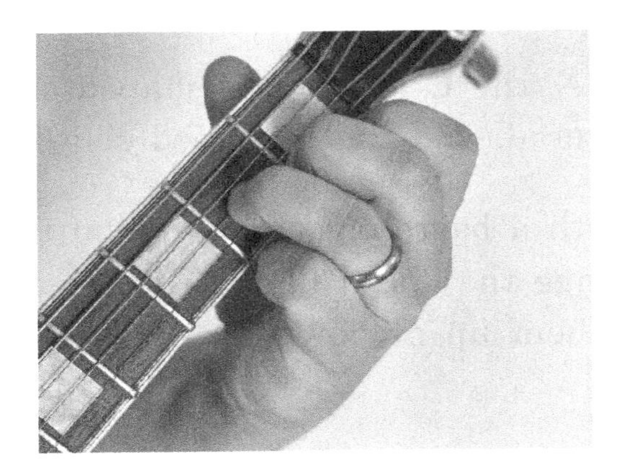

Emin7

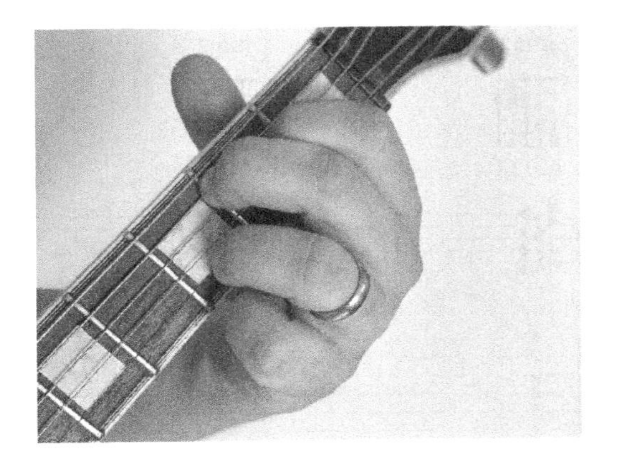

Fmin7

Movable Maj7th's and Min7th's

Delving further into what makes barre chords special, is that their shapes can be transferred anywhere across the neck to create new root chords. This is what's called movable chords.

Three of these — the A, the C and the D-shaped chords — are based on the root chords we covered, and the E-shaped chord is a variation.

They are all played with a barre or semi-barre on the 2nd fret. Changing the root note will change the chord name; therefore, as with all movable chords, simply move them up or down the neck to play the exact chord you need.

A Root shape	C shape (Root on A string)	D Root shape	E Root shape
Bmaj7	Dmaj7	Emaj7	F♯maj7
12341	43111	1234	1 342

TAB	Bmaj7	Dmaj7	Emaj7	F♯maj7
1	2	2	4	
2	4	2	4	2
3	3	2	4	3
4	4	4	2	3
5	2	5		x
6				2

Bmaj7 — A Root Moveable Position — 2nd fret

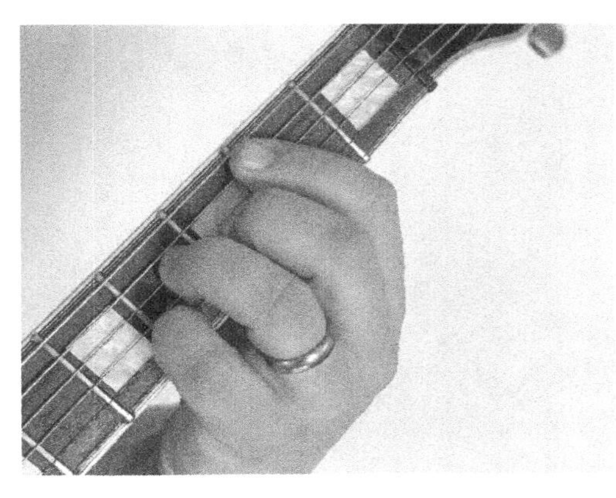

Dmaj7 — D shape — Root on D string — Moveable Position — 2nd fret

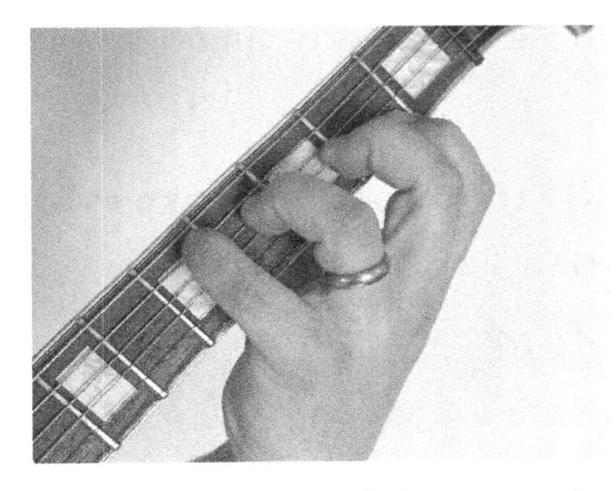

Emaj7 — A Root Moveable Position — 2nd fret

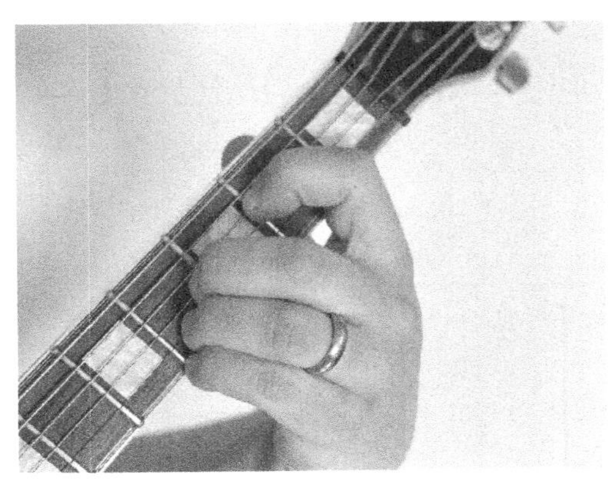

F#maj7 — E Root Moveable Position — 2nd fret

Let's re-examine our good ole friend, the chord progression...

We'll start with an exercise that really highlights the distinctive sound of the Maj7th.

Exercise #83 — Maj7th Chord Progression 1

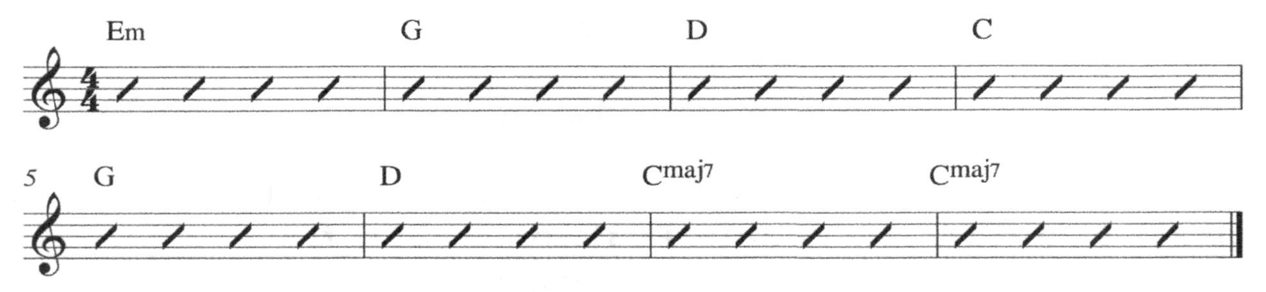

Refer back to Exercise #42 — Rhythm Pattern 9 — 4/4 for the rhythm I'd like you to play here.

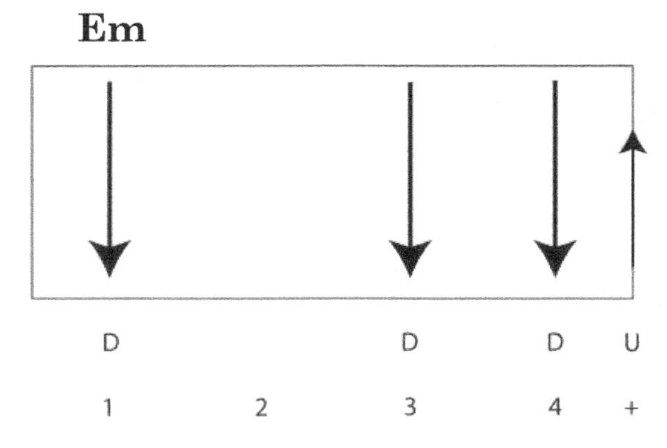

This is actually the chord progression used in the song "Country Feed" by REM, from their album Out of Time. Play along with the rhythm above and you'll get the vibe and the sound of this song uses the Maj7th chord to great effect.

Another great song that uses a Cmaj7 is "My Friends" by Red Hot Chili Peppers. It can be found alternating with the Asus2 chord during the chorus.

Another good use of the Cmaj7 chord is a chord progression similar to the one used in Something" by The Beatles.

Exercise #84 — Maj7th Chord Progression 2

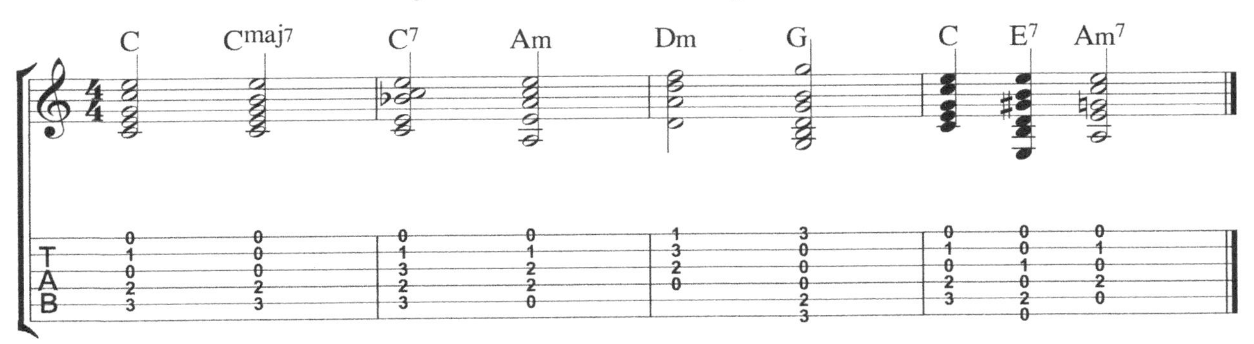

We'll follow this up with another nice simple chord progression to get that Am7 down.

Exercise #85 — Min7th Chord Progression 1

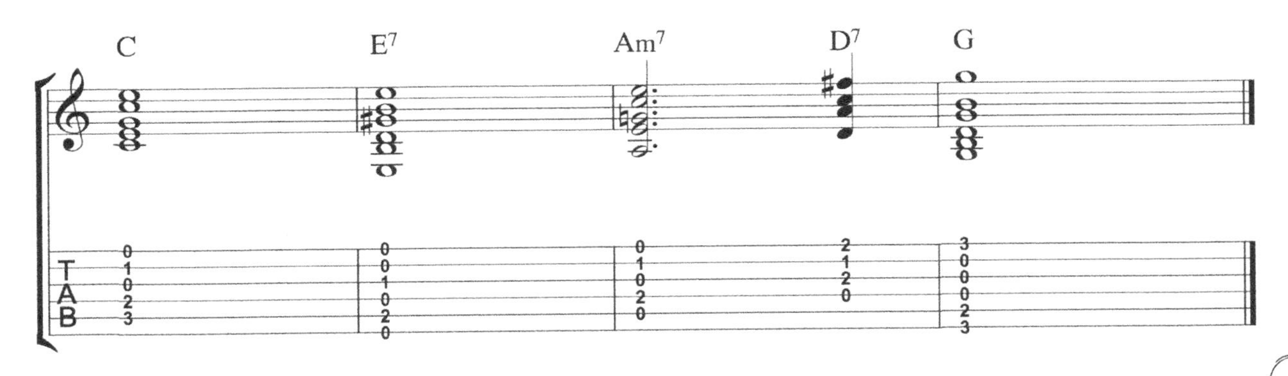

Exercise #86 — Maj7th Chord Progression 3

Next up we have another all TIME classic...

This and the final progression are going to be quite a bit harder due to their use of barre chords. You didn't think they were going away, did you? Nope, barre chords are an essential part of mastering the guitar—so let's get the hang of them with some more exercises!

Do you recognize the song of this chord progression? I gave you a pretty obvious clue up above...

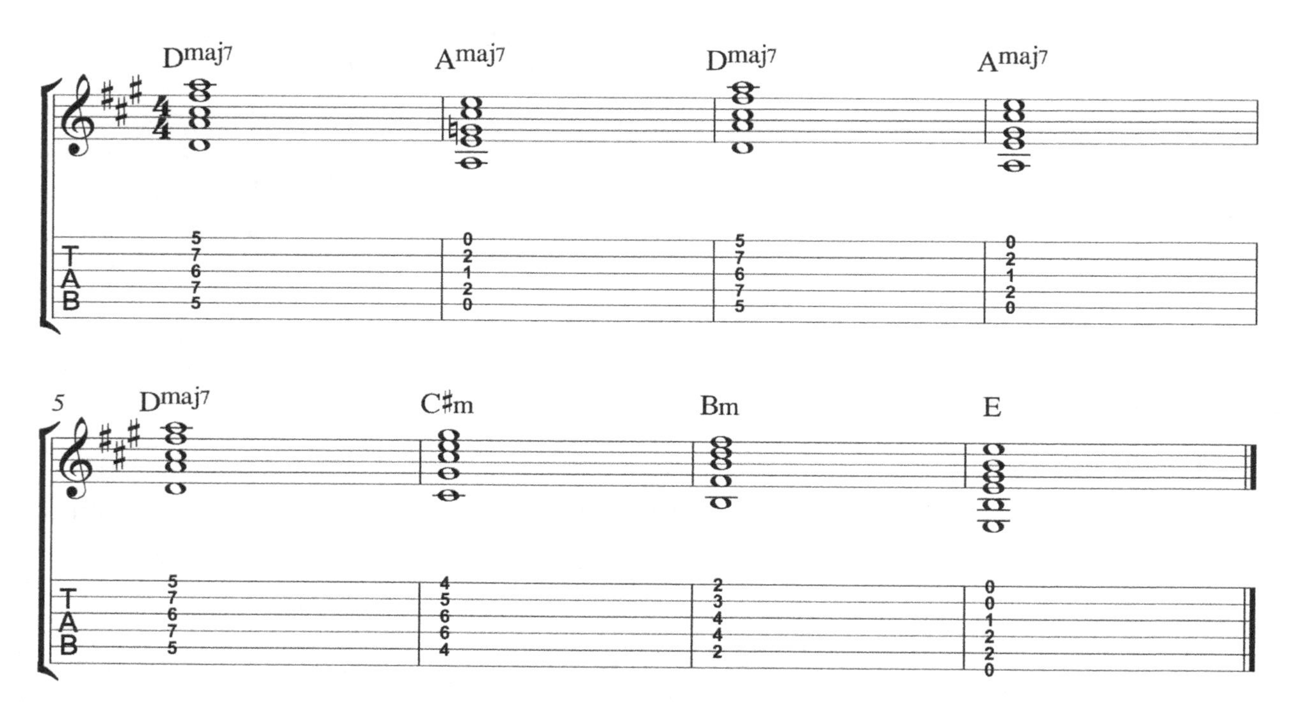

That's right, it's the interlude section of "Time" by Pink Floyd.

Finally, for Maj7th and Min7ths in well-known songs, we're going back to the Chili Peppers for a truly iconic use of the Major 7th chord. It's played at the end of the verse chord progression of their classic song "Under the Bridge".

The chord is an Emaj7 played using the moveable A root shape on the 7th fret, and it offers a wonderful sustaining resolution to the verse chord progression that is repeated before it.

The verse chords are shown below; these are interspersed with numerous Hendrix-inspired fills, along with the fantastic Emaj7 at the end.

Exercise #87 — Maj7th Chord Progression 4

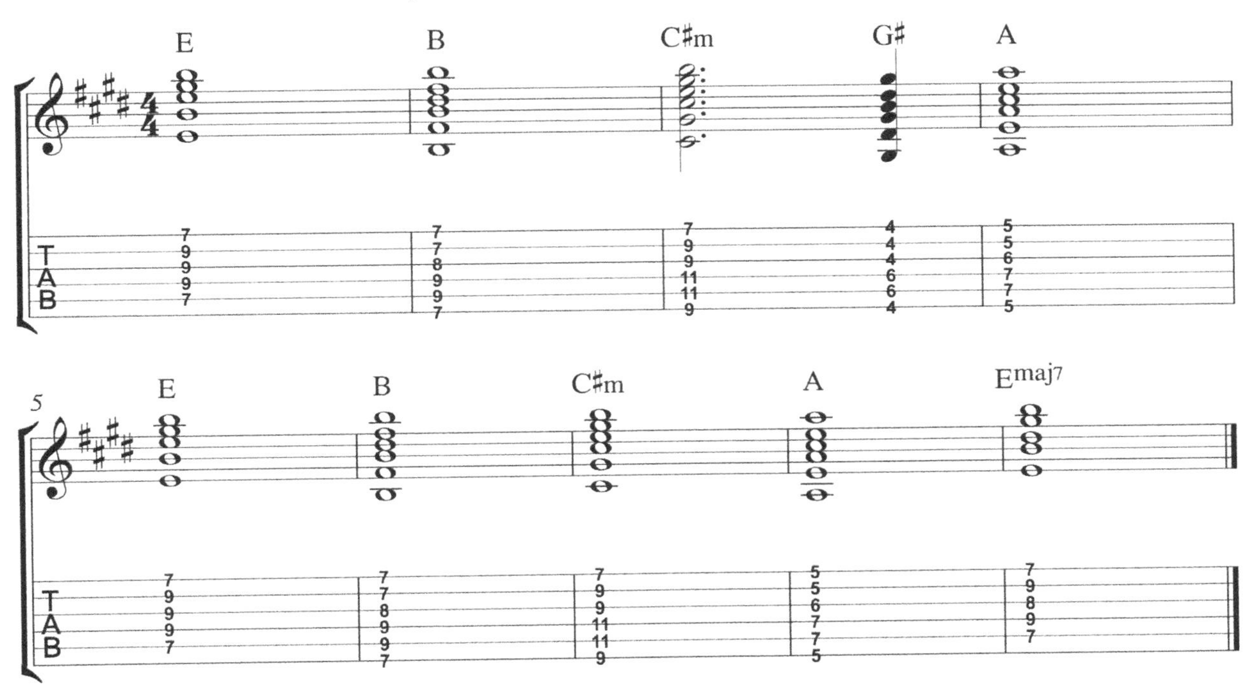

More Uses of the Maj7th in Pop Music

Even though it's a wonderful sounding chord, it really isn't used that often in pop and rock songs. More examples include "Roxanne" by The Police, "Rain Song" by Led Zeppelin, "Down by the River" by Neil Young, and "Ferry Cross the Mersey" by Jerry and the Pacemakers.

But where you'll really find both the maj7th and min7th chords used extensively is in jazz, so...

Let's Get Jazzy!

This is where major and minor sevenths really come into their own — the wonderful world of Jazz!

The **II-V-I progression** is the most popular chord progression in jazz. In fact, it's almost impossible to find a jazz standard that doesn't use it somewhere in the song. Some songs might *only* contain this progression from start to finish.

It's featured in countless tunes, in every key — including many different permutations, both harmonically and rhythmically. For this reason, we'll show a few different variations of it in different positions using various chord shapes.

Exercise #88 — Jazz Maj7th and Min7th Chord Progression 1

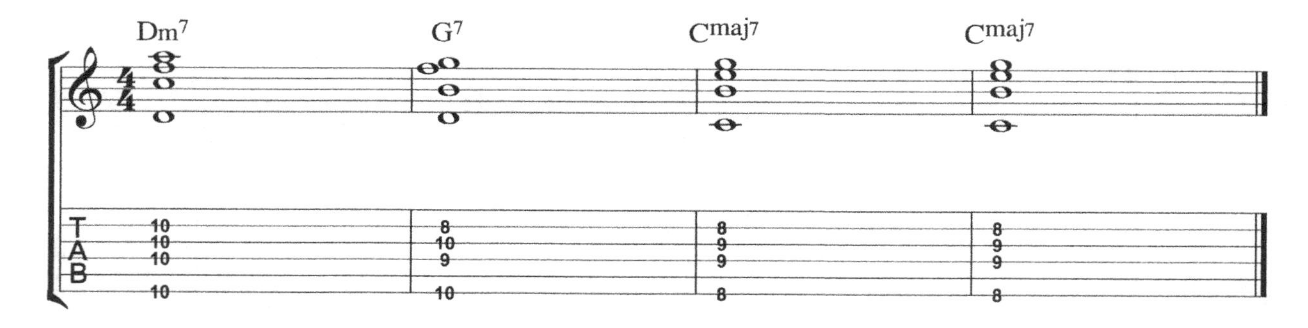

If you're not familiar with playing jazz chords, these may be a bit of a stretch for your fingers. However, as far as jazz chords go, they're quite basic--so if jazz is your thing, or you want to explore the complexities of Maj7ths and Min7ths more, this is a great place to start.

Exercise #89 — Jazz Maj7th and Min7th Chord Progression 2

Dm7 G7 Cmaj7 Cmaj7

Exercise #90 — Jazz Maj7th and Min7th Chord Progression 3

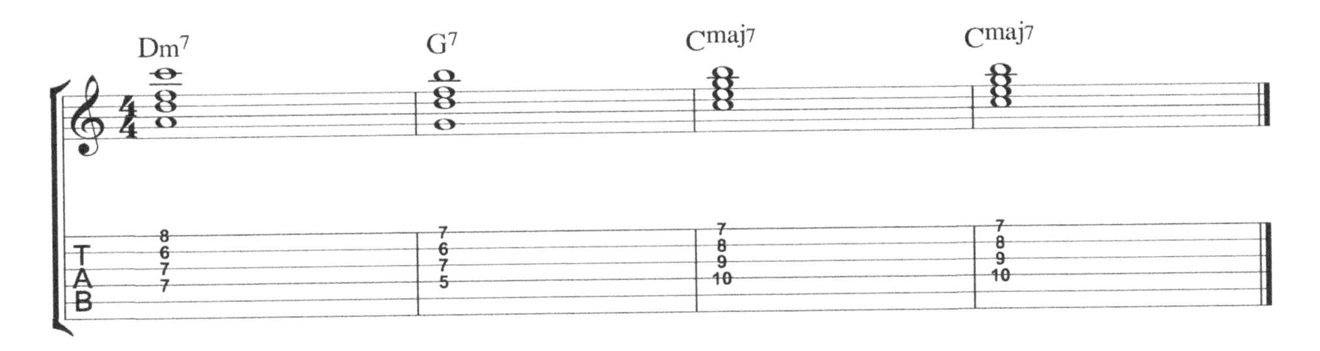

> *"Regardless of what you play, the biggest thing is keeping the feel going."*
>
> *Wes Montgomery,*
> *arguably the greatest jazz guitarist of all time.*

CHAPTER 8

Let's End with Some Songs!

At this point, I'd like to reiterate that it is indeed possible to dramatically improve your guitar playing skills with just 10 minutes a day of devoted practice.

Yes, I've thrown a lot at you in the span of one book. I don't expect you to have everything mastered right away. Work at your own pace--and cover only what you feel ready to tackle. But stick with it.

10 minutes daily. That's it. You could run through a scale pattern while watching Netflix. You can practice hammer-ons after your morning coffee. Before going to bed, take 10 minutes and memorize the C Major chord shape across the fretboard.

These exercises are designed to stay with you throughout your entire playing career. Always refer back to them, no matter how advanced your skills become down the road. The greatest players in the world always work to improve themselves!

Having said that, the real reason you want to be a better player is so you can play some actual songs — right?!

So, what better way to finish off this book than with some classic songs for you to perfect your chops on!

Let's start with...

Exercise #91 — Chord Progression 1 — 4/4

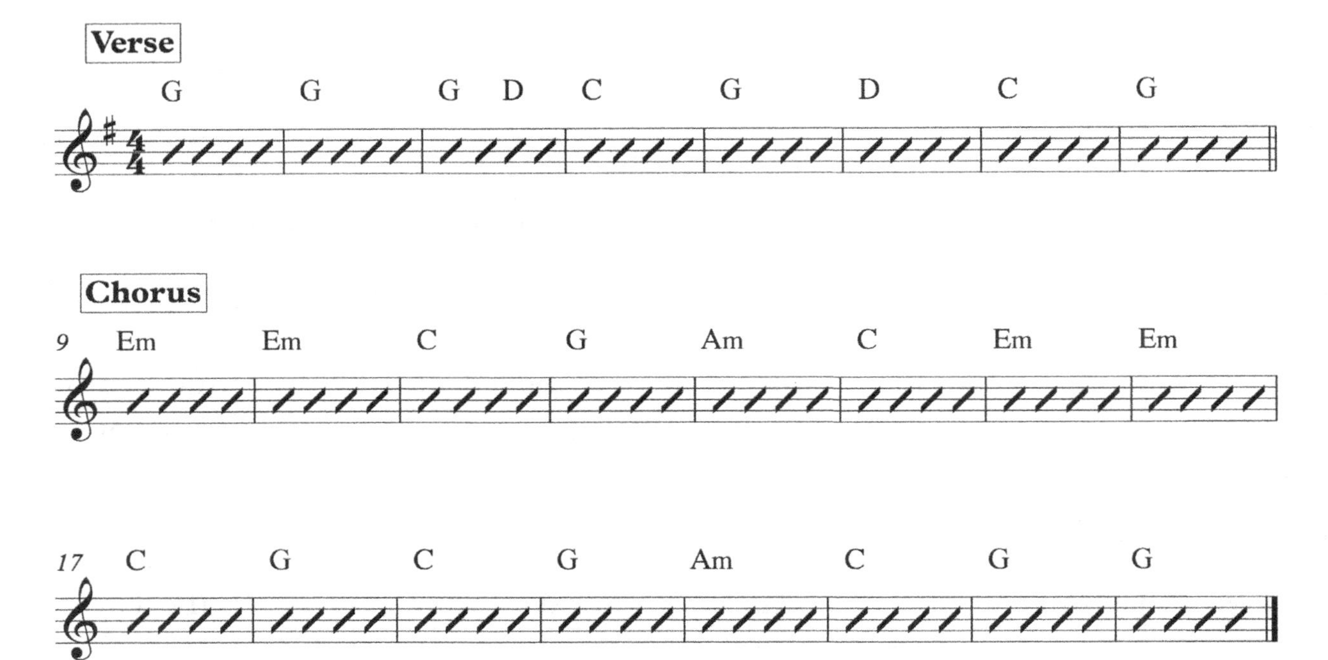

We'll start with a simple country-rock chord progression that can be played with any of the 4/4 rhythm patterns included in the book. But it works very well with Exercise #40 — Rhythm Pattern 7, which is shown again below:

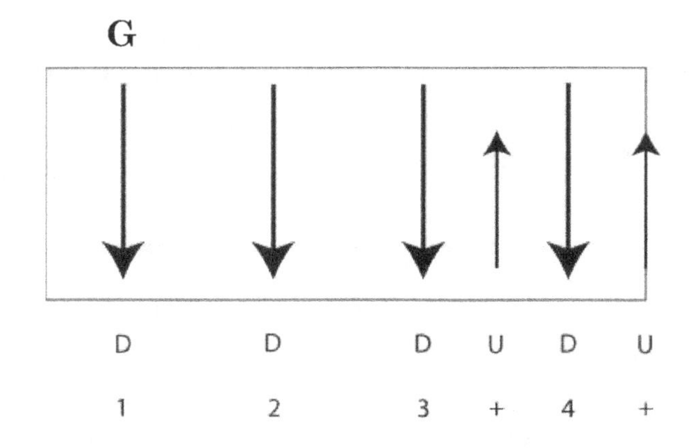

This progression shouldn't cause you any difficulties — plus it's a good workout for your strumming arm. Keep it going and get that folky country swing into the feel of the song.

Exercise #92 — Chord Progression 2 — 4/4

This is in the style of "Shallow" by Lady Gaga and Bradley Cooper. Simple chords and a simple rhythm, so you shouldn't have any problem with this one. It is well worth playing along with the song as well. This increases your skills by making you practice every part of the song, and it gets you used to playing along with a real band.

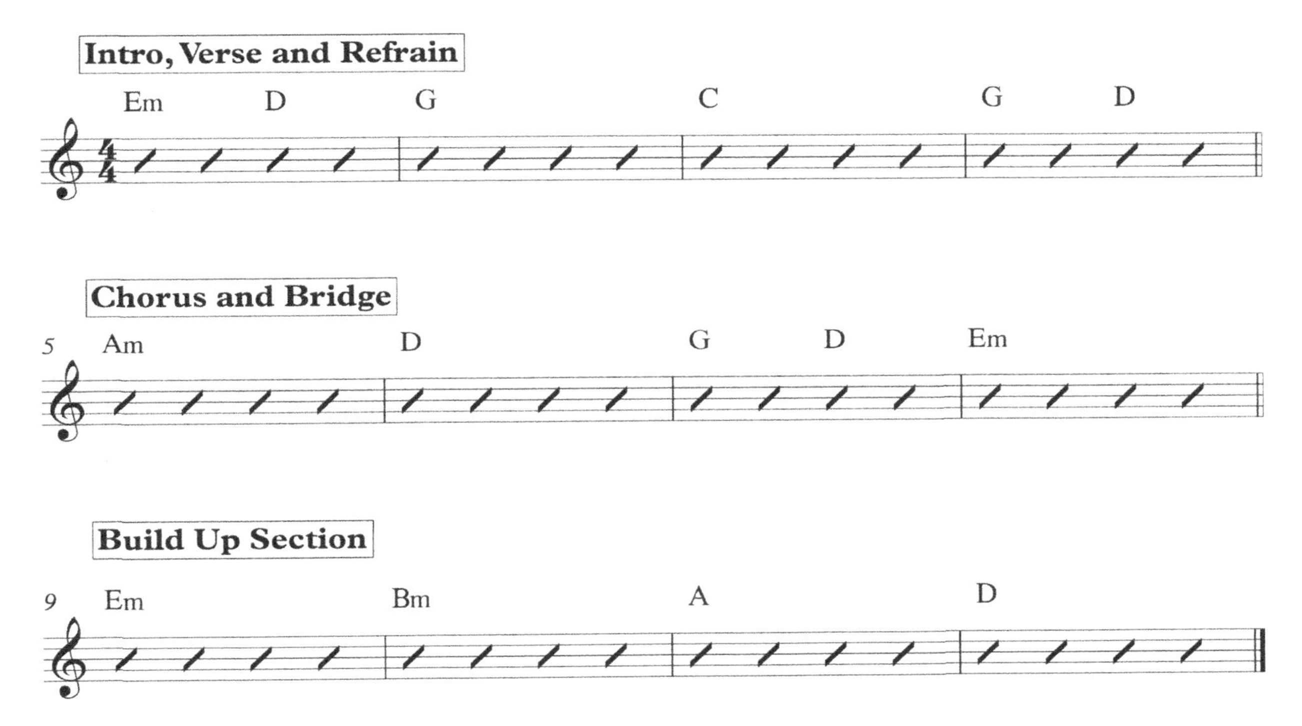

Exercise #93 — Chord Progression 3 — 4/4

The next progression is Jimi Hendrix's version of "Hey Joe". This is again a simple song with an equally easy chord progression from the most innovative guitarist of all time.

No one is 100% sure who wrote it, and a number of people have claimed it as their own unsuccessfully. Hendrix always played it as a cover--and even though he most definitely didn't write it, his version is by far the most famous.

The chords should present you with no problems; it's just a case of getting the "funky muscle" in your strumming arm going to get the Hendrix swing, which is no easy task. Then there are all the delicious fills to add, but that's for another book I'm afraid.

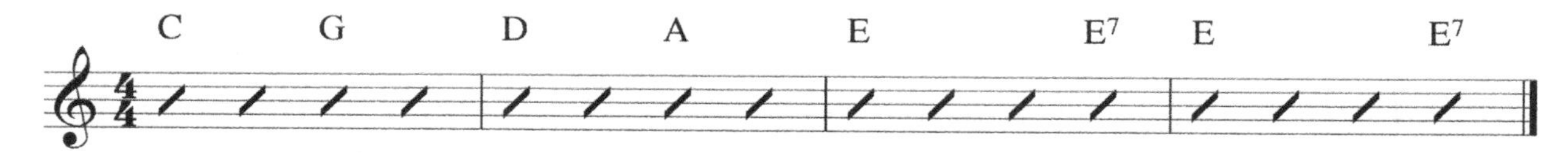

Exercise #94 — Chord Progression 4 — 4/4

Our next progression is in the style of "Here Comes The Sun" by The Beatles, which was written by George Harrison and appeared on their 1969 album Abbey Road.

It's quite a complicated picking pattern with some added notes, but if you play around with adding a few notes to these chords and picking them, you may be surprised with how close to the original you can make it sound.

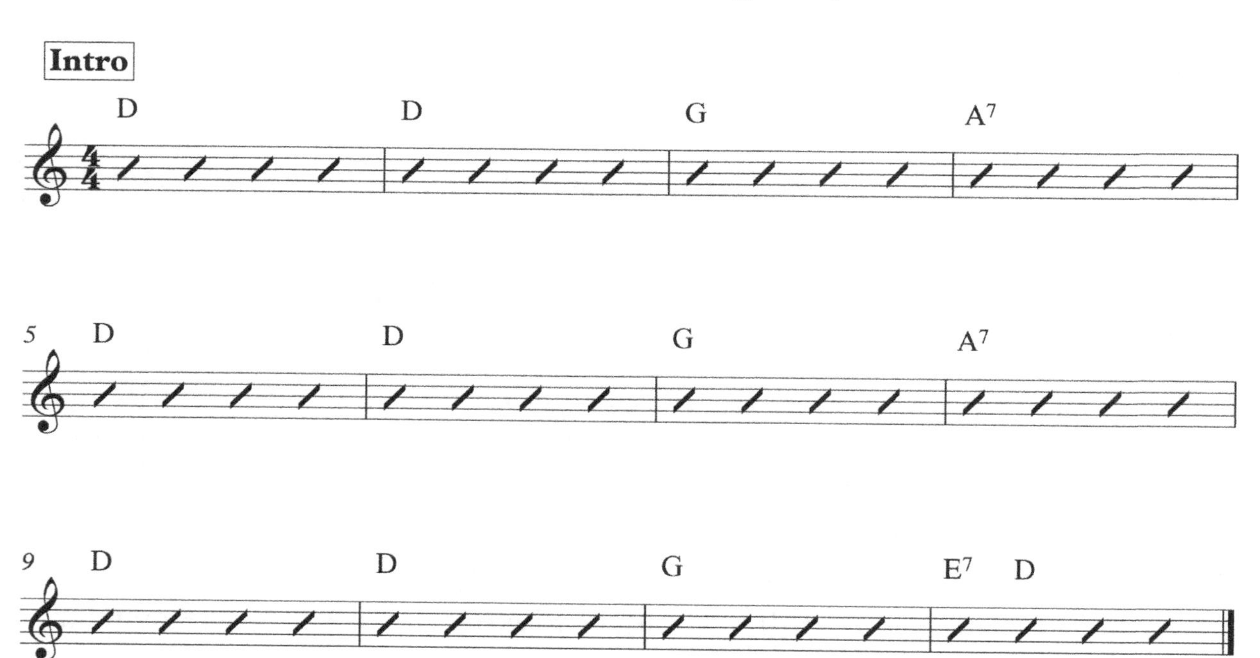

Exercise #95 — Chord Progression 5 — 4/4

Next up, we have a classic 12-bar in the key of A. It's quite unbelievable how many Blues songs are structured in exactly this way; the key may change, but the relationship between the chords does not.

Not only does the structure not change from song to song, but it doesn't normally change within the song either. So, you basically play this exact same sequence from start to finish.

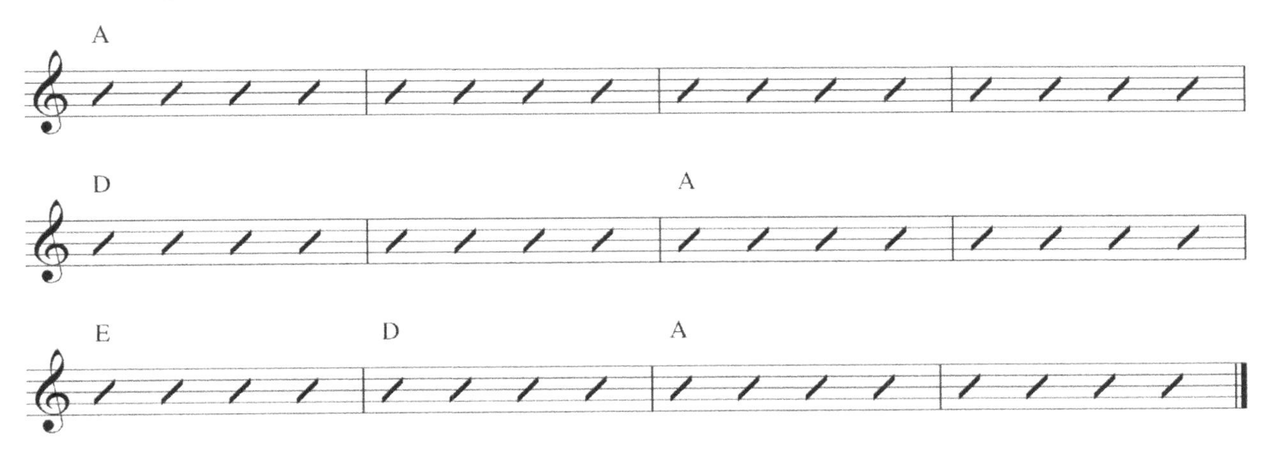

To make it sound far more "bluesy", try playing the following riffs over the chord progressions:

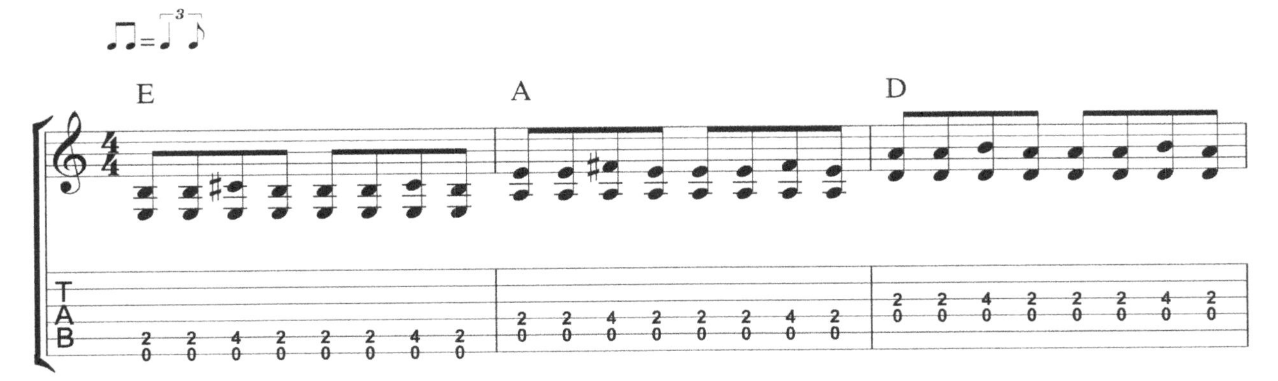

Or how about a slow blues...

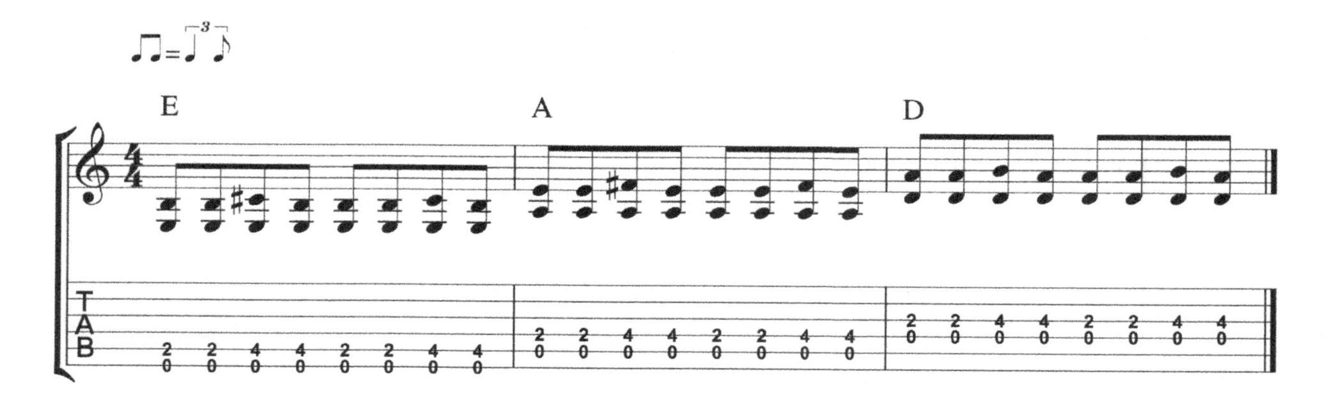

Exercise #96 — Chord Progression 6 — 4/4

In this progression we take a look at a typical chord change that has been used in various songs, regardless of genre. It's a very popular change where **I** chord moves to the **II7**.

In bar 3, the C major chord goes to D7th, which is the II degree of the scale. It then moves to the dominant 7th. This is an example of "Modal interchange".

Many tunes across different genres have used this change. Stevie Wonder's "Isn't She Lovely", jazz standard "Take the A train", or Bossa Nova classic "Girl from Ipanema" all contain this change.

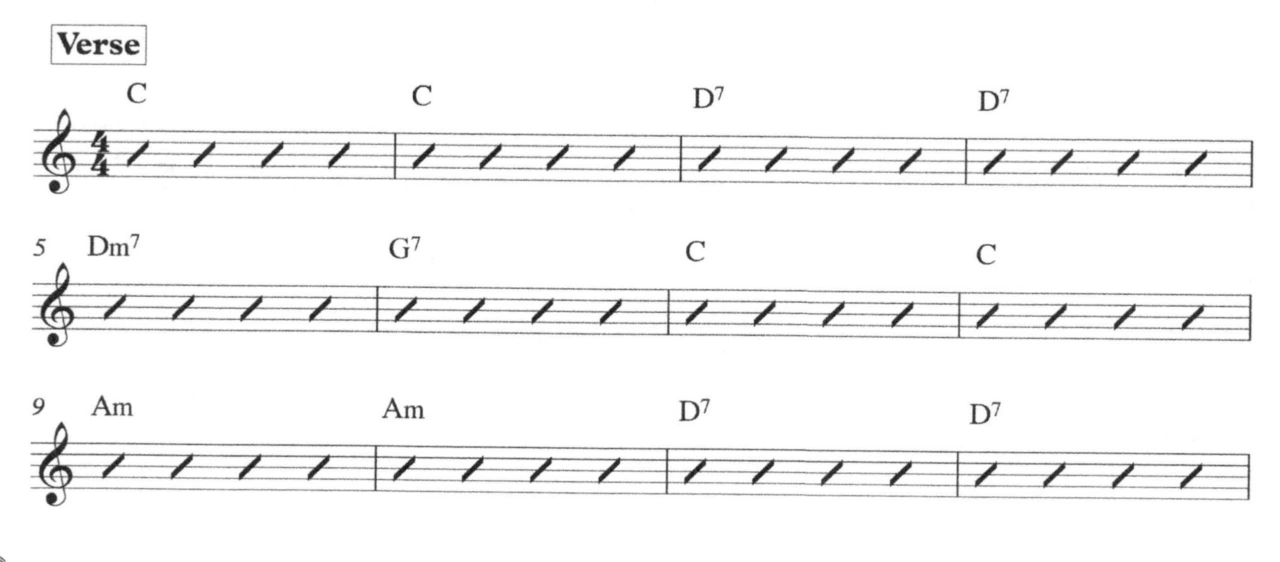

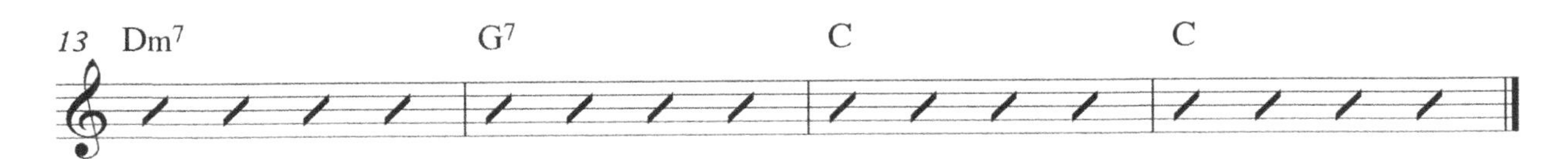

Exercise #97 — Chord Progression 7 — 4/4

Let's now try another minor chord progression, which sounds great when picked. You can use the same picking pattern we've just featured or any one you think sounds good with the song. It sounds particularly good if you pick it quickly.

Of course, it also works well when strummed, so choose any of the strumming patterns we've featured and strum away to your heart's content.

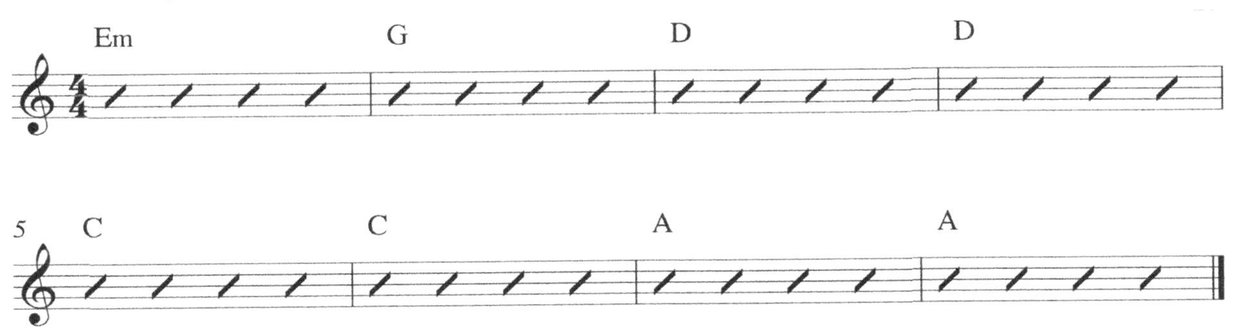

Exercise #98 — Chord Progression 8 — 4/4

From picking to lots of downstrums, let's now take a look at what has become known as the Pop-punk Chord Progression.

This, as the name suggests, is commonly used by Pop-punk bands such as Green Day and Blink 182. But it's also featured in songs as diverse as "Crying" by Aerosmith, "Already Gone" by Kelly Clarkson, and "Down Under" by Men at Work.

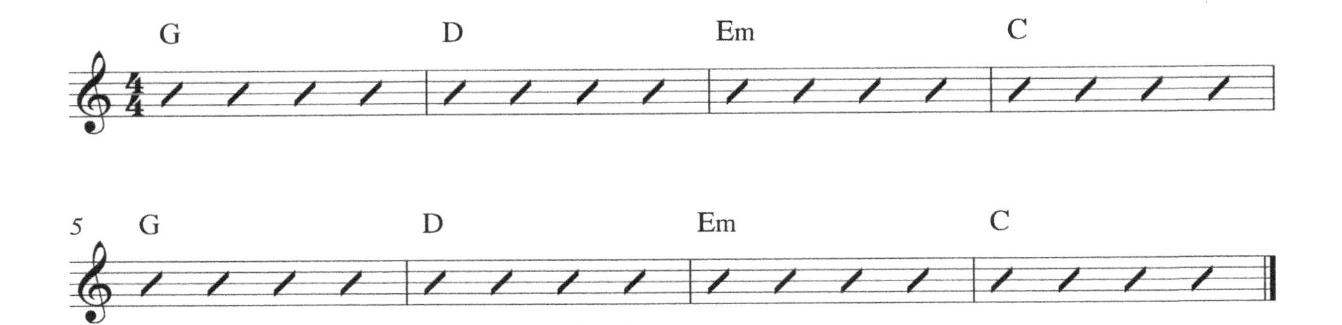

It can be played in any number of keys; I chose G for this example. When played by pop-punk bands, they normally use power chords--either muted or unmuted--depending on the feel of the song.

The rhythm pattern is all downstrokes, as was shown in Exercise #38, which is repeated below:

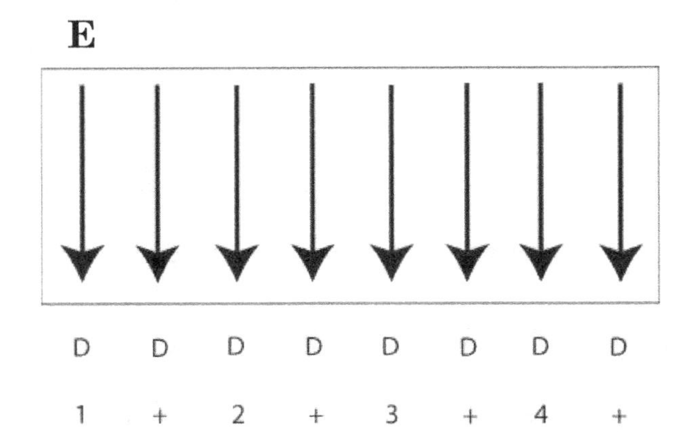

Exercise #99 — Chord Progression 9 — 4/4

Now let's take a little stroll through time, all the way back to the 1950s... This progression was widely used back then in the Doo-Wop genre — and can be found in songs such as "Monster Mash" by Boris Picket and "The Book of Love" by The Monotones.

Since then, it has been widely used by artists who were inspired by music from that era, including Adele and Amy Winehouse, as well as bands of all genres from U2 to Bruno Mars.

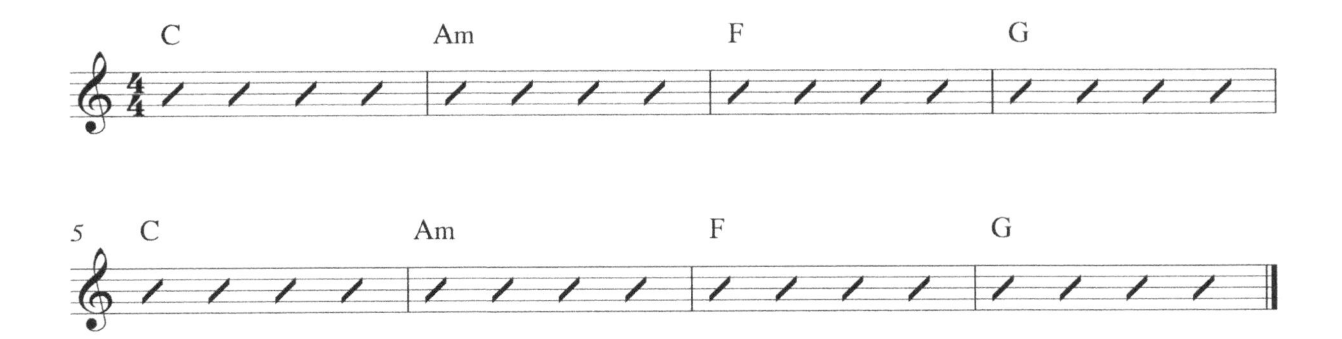

In terms of rhythm patterns, the choice is yours — this progression sounds good with all of them, which is why it has lasted for such a long time and is still widely used today.

Exercise #100 — Chord Progression 10 — 6/8

For our final exercise, let's end with a progression that I'm sure you've heard before... It's been around since at least the beginning of the twentieth century, with the first written version being in 1925. However, certain parts of the song date back much further to English and American folk songs.

No one knows exactly who wrote it, but it's been covered by numerous artists including Bob Dylan, Dolly Parton, The Animals, Frijid Pink and Sinead O'Connor.

It is played in 6/8, which means you need to play the second rhythm pattern we covered — Exercise #35 — two times in every bar. It's also played much faster than you might imagine. Just take a listen to The Animals recording and you will hear how fast it is played.

This makes it a fantastic rhythm workout for your strumming arm. The rhythm may be simple, but to play it at a consistently fast rate throughout the whole song will take quite a bit of effort and practice.

No sense ending on an easy note, right?

This Is the End, Beautiful Friend

Well, here we are. The end. You've come a long way since the beginning of this book...

Some the exercises you've learned will help improve your skills over time, some of them will inspire you to make up new and harder versions yourself as time goes on, and there are even some that you will use for the rest of your life as superb warm-up exercises.

Everything you need to significantly improve your playing is included somewhere in this book. Take your time with it—and remember to get as much out of every exercise as you can by playing it slowly to start with and making sure that everything is absolutely perfect. Then add in a metronome or drum machine at a slow speed and play with that. Then increase the speed as you master the exercise.

If you follow everything in this book, your playing is guaranteed to improve. Just 10 minutes at a time—you really don't need any more than that.

And remember, we all play guitar to have fun! So have FUN with these exercises, with your practicing, and with every mesmerizing performance of your career!

When you're done, put the guitar back on its stand — and remember that...

> *"Sometimes the nicest thing to do with a guitar is just look at it."*
>
> *Thom Yorke, Radiohead*

What Next?

Now that you've mastered the 100 guitar exercises, the world is your oyster! Go out there and learn a lot of licks, play a lot of songs and create some amazing music! It will take time and there is a lot of work to put in. But isn't that the beauty of music? The Journey.

We appreciate your trust in us through the course of this book. And we would love to be a part of your journey going forward too.

If you've gotten the exercises in this book under your belt and are looking for advanced guitar exercises, I suggest our next feature for you.

Guitar Exercises: 10x Guitar Skills in 10 Minutes a Day

We have a 100 more exercises which can take you to the next level of guitar playing in no time. Speed it up or slow it down — with this book, it's all up to you.

You can grab a copy on our website.

Farewell!

Psssstttt....

What are you doing here? Are you lost?

Do people even look at the last pages of a book?

Jokes aside, I hope you enjoyed this book. I certainly loved the process of writing it.

If you enjoyed this book, could you take 2 minutes to leave a review about it?

Reviews are the lifeblood for small publishers and help us get our books into the hands of more guitarists like you.

We read every review personally and appreciate each one of it.

To leave a review, simply go to the platform you purchased the book from and type in your review.

With that said, here's Guitar Head signing off!

Until next time then? I'll see you in another book.

THE END

Made in the USA
Las Vegas, NV
30 March 2024